Write Back Soon!

Letters of Love and Encouragement to Young Women

MARGARET D. NADAULD

BOOKCRAFT

Salt Lake City, Utah

Library of Congress Cataloging-in-Publication Data

Nadauld, Margaret D., 1944–
  Write back soon! : letters of love and encouragement to young women / Margaret D. Nadauld.
    p. cm.
  Includes bibliographical references and index.
  ISBN 1-57345-955-0
    1. Teenage girls—Religious life. 2. Young women—Religious life. 3. Christian life—Mormon authors. I. Title.
BX8643.Y6 N33 2001
248.8'33—dc21   2001016175

Printed in the United States of America   72082-6808
10 9   8   7   6   5   4   3   2   1

To R. Morgan and Helen B. Dyreng,

my parents,

whose example and love inspire me.

contents

✧ a c k n o w l e d g m e n t s ✧

It has been a joy to work on this project. I am grateful to Sheri Dew, my friend with whom I serve, for suggesting to me the idea of a book; to Stephen, my dear husband, for his continual encouragement, interest, and inspiration; to our seven sons: Stephen, Justen, James, Lincoln, Taylor, Adam, and Aaron, who have always given me another point of view and who are bringing beautiful daughters into our family: Stacy, Susan, Rebecca, and Lindsay so far; and to young women everywhere, who give me hope for the future, who have so much promise, and whom I love. A heartfelt thank you to Melissa M. Jorgensen for her encouragement and help in organizing this project in the early stages; to Jennifer Dimick for her enthusiasm and skill in typing the manuscript; to Janna DeVore and Emily Watts for their thoughtful care in editing; and to Sheryl Dickert and Tom Hewitson for their beautiful, creative design of this book.

Dear Reader,

I frequently receive letters from young women. You bear testimony in your letters, you ask questions, you tell me what you worry about. And often you close by saying, "Write back soon!" How I would love to become a pen pal to every young woman! *Write Back Soon* is my endeavor to do just that.

This book is a collection of letters written to a young woman I have chosen to call Elizabeth. She is not just one girl, but a composite of the many precious girls I have heard from. It is my hope that in reading these letters, you—my delightful, precious young teenage sister—will find personal insights and answers to your own questions.

I hope as you read you will gain a better understanding of your eternal and divine potential. I hope you will believe that you are Heavenly Father's daughter. You were His child even before you were born and will continue as such after this earth experience. You are His eternally. He knows you and loves you more than you can comprehend. Our Heavenly Father wants you to succeed and He will help you. That is what His plan, the gospel, is all about. Because of its possibilities and promises, the gospel is often called the great plan of happiness, and you are an important, essential part of this great plan.

After reading each letter, I hope you will take the time to respond. Study the verses of scripture mentioned in the letters. Record your thoughts in this book or in your personal journal. Share your testimony in writing, then read over it many times to remember how you feel when touched by the Spirit. It is my sincere prayer that through these pages you will come to have a better understanding of who you really are, what you can become, and what you can do to make your life a masterpiece.

May you find some joy and direction as you share in these letters.

With love from your friend, your cheerleader, your sister,
Margaret D. Nadauld

chapter one

Hooray! It's a Girl!

"we are daughters of our Heavenly Father"

Dear Elizabeth,

Thank you for the sensitive and insightful letter you wrote to me. Since I received it I have thought about you a great deal. I would love to get to know you better! I have wondered what you think about, what you like to do, and what you want to be. I have wondered what your parents are like and what you have been taught. What are your friends like, what about the boys you know? What do you think about the television programs you see? What do you do after school?

Do you go to church, Elizabeth? I hope you do, and I hope you like the way you feel when you are there.

Thank you for asking me to "write back soon." I would love to! What a great invitation! I hope that you will continue to write to me and share some thoughts and ideas. Your letter was the greatest!

I wanted to share with you right away the most exciting thing

that happened the other day. The phone rang and I ran to it expectantly because I'd been waiting for an important call. And here it was! Our married son, Justen, was on the other end, and he spoke almost reverently as the words tumbled out: "Mom, she's here! We have a baby girl, and she is beautiful! You will love her. When can you and Dad come?"

After I quit cheering, "Hooray! Hooray! It's a Girl!" over and over quite a few times, I tried to regain my composure and calmly say, "Congratulations, son. We're on our way! But first, tell me all about her."

Frankly, I stumbled over the feminine pronoun "her," and when it came out it was spoken almost in awe. You see, I had never used words like "she" and "her" in reference to a new baby in our family in all thirty years of our marriage. I am the mother of seven boys! There are no girls. On top of that, each grandchild has been a beautiful, amazing, precious, little boy. We know boys. In our family we do boys. They are the greatest! But a *girl*—now that is a new experience. What do you do with a girl?

We could hardly wait to find out! It didn't take us long to load up the car and head straight for Sun Valley, where this little one had made her entrance into the world. After a fairly speedy four-hour drive we screeched to a stop in front of the small-town hospital, jumped from the car, sprinted to the front door, and hurried down the short hallway and into the new mother's room. Can you tell that we were excited? We loved and hugged new-mom-Susan, and then she quietly pointed to a small hospital bassinet close beside her.

And there she was! A brand-new little baby girl. As we drew close and looked at her for the first time, our hearts overflowed with gratitude for the miracle of birth. It was with a feeling of reverence that we tenderly moved aside the soft blanket and got our first look at our own little miracle. A precious baby. A tiny girl. A gift from God, straight from heaven.

When I first held this new baby girl in my arms, I could hardly

see her pretty little face through the tears in my eyes. They were tears of thanksgiving welling up from a grateful heart. To this little one, so soon from the arms of God, I whispered the words of a song:

> Do you know who you are, little child of mine?
> So precious and dear to me?
> Do you know you're a part of a great design
> That is vast as eternity?[1]

Oh, Elizabeth, I wonder if this little infant girl can somehow recall the lessons she learned in the world of spirits as she prepared to come down to earth. William Wordsworth wrote a wonderful poem, part of which talks about our coming to earth.

> Our birth is but a sleep and a forgetting:
> The Soul that rises with us, our life's Star,
> Hath had elsewhere its setting,
> And cometh from afar:
> Not in entire unforgetfulness,
> And not in utter nakedness,
> But trailing clouds of glory do we come
> From God, who is our home.[2]

As we grow, we forget what we knew before our birth. You and I can't remember what we were taught in heaven because a veil has been drawn across our understanding. It is part of the plan of our Heavenly Father to send us here to earth to walk by faith. But the scriptures and latter-day prophets teach us some things about that pre-earth life which are really important to know.

For example, you were prepared before this world was to come to earth in the due time of the Lord to do some very unusual and wonderful things! The Doctrine and Covenants teaches that the noble and great ones, "even before they were born, . . . with many others, received their first lessons in the world of spirits and were prepared to come forth in the due time of the Lord to labor in his vineyard for the

salvation of the souls of men" (D&C 138:56). Did you know that? What a wonderful thing to know about your mission on earth.

Our Heavenly Father has given you the magnificent gift of life. He sent you here to earth for a purpose and He wants you to succeed. He will help you. For He says, "This is my work and my glory—to bring to pass the immortality and eternal life of man" (Moses 1:39). The whole purpose of the Savior's mission to earth was to show us the way to live our lives, to set an example. And, in addition, to help us get back on the right track if we make a mistake. He paid the price for our mistakes. That, of course, is what the Atonement is, and sincere repentance on our part makes it possible for His sacrifice to work in our lives. I am so thankful for that great plan! I'm also thankful that Heavenly Father gives us parents and others who love us who will show us the right way to live and help us be successful.

Elizabeth, when you have time, take just a moment and ask someone who was there in the early days of your life all about your arrival on earth. And then think of all those who have loved you. What were their hopes and dreams for your life? I would love to hear all about it, so write soon!

With thanks for new life, bright futures, and with love,

Your friend

God's Gift to You

"you will be . . . even irresistible"

Dear Elizabeth,

Thank you for writing. I loved hearing about your earliest days on earth and those who were part of it. It's fun to know how our stories begin.

I'm still in awe of our new baby girl. She's so cute! As I held her in my arms, I moved aside the soft new blanket to see her tiny little fingers and toes, and then I took soft white stockings out of my pocket and put them on her little baby feet. The stockings were too big for her, even though they were the smallest size available. They had exquisite lace on them—never appropriate for the boy babies I've known and loved so well for so long.

This was a first . . . a girl! She was different from the boys. We used words like "her," "she," "lovely," and "pretty."

We will help her understand that she was feminine and female

long before her physical body began to develop inside her mother. Did you know that, Elizabeth? The spirit that gives life to your body is female. In other words, you are "all girl!"

You are all girl from the inside out, your spirit *and* your body. Prophets teach us that important concept. In the Proclamation on the Family we are taught that our "gender is an essential characteristic of individual premortal, mortal, and eternal identity and purpose." Truly, one of your finest gifts from God is your divine, feminine nature.

Elizabeth, I hope that you love being a girl. Thank Heavenly Father for the privilege of being born to womanhood, for it is a divine and priceless blessing. Your Father in Heaven has blessed you, His daughter, with some very precious qualities in extra capacity.

President James E. Faust teaches young women that "One of your unique, precious, and sublime gifts is your femininity, with its natural grace, goodness, and divinity. . . . One of your particular gifts is your feminine intuition. Do not limit yourselves. As you seek to know the will of Heavenly Father in your life and become more spiritual, you will be far more attractive, even irresistible. You can use your smiling loveliness to bless those you love and all you meet, and spread great joy. Femininity is part of the God-given divinity within each of you. It is your incomparable power and influence to do good. You can, through your supernal gifts, bless the lives of children, women, and men. Be proud of your womanhood. Enhance it. Use it to serve others."[1]

President Faust is right! As a girl, you have great capacity for goodness. Do you fully understand the greatness of your gifts and talents and the importance of developing them to bless mankind? Your gifts are unique and precious. Femininity shows itself differently in each girl or woman, but each one possesses it. It is part of your inner beauty and strength and nobility.

With all the opportunities and choices you will have on this earth, I so hope that most of all you will be thankful that you are

female. I hope you will honor that special divine gift from God. For it is a gift that can bless many lives for good, forever.

President Gordon B. Hinckley has spoken another very tender truth. "Woman is God's supreme creation," he tells us. "Only after the earth had been formed, after the day had been separated from the night, after the waters had been divided from the land, after vegetation and animal life had been created, and after man had been placed on the earth, was woman created; and only then was the work pronounced complete and good."[2]

Now that should make you feel very special Elizabeth! Stay close to Heavenly Father so He can guide you in the development of the unique gifts He has given you. I'd love to have you write to me about some of the divine, "even irresistible" feminine gifts you see in yourself. What opportunities do you have to develop those special gifts? Have you thought about how you can use those gifts to bless others?

With joy in the divine gift of being "all girl,"

Your sister

chapter three

A Name and a Blessing

what's in a name?

Dear Elizabeth,

You have such a pretty name. I think it is one of the loveliest in the language. I've also been intrigued by your last name. Do you know its origin? Are your ancestors German or Mexican? What do you know about your ancestors? Are there any "lost sheep" in your family?

Let me tell you why I've been thinking about names. Remember the baby girl I've been writing to you about? Last Sunday she received her name and blessing in sacrament meeting. It was a day her parents had looked forward to and prepared for since her birth. Her mother had her dress all prepared and waiting. It was white and long and had lots of lace. It was beautiful! It flowed several inches past her skinny little legs. She didn't wear the stockings with lace at the ankles I put on her feet the day she was born; she went barefoot! Her uncle, who stood in the circle for the blessing, had her binky in his pocket. If she

cried, he was prepared to pop it in her mouth. But she didn't make a peep.

Most important of all, more important than the dress and the binky, her thankful father gave her a name and blessing. She received the first priesthood ordinance in her life. How do you like the name chosen for her: Estelle Elizabeth? I think that middle name is pretty special, don't you? I wonder what her friends will call her?

In the blessing, she was told of her precious worth. Her father blessed her to be a girl who loves her Heavenly Father, a girl who will honor her parents and be good to her brother, a girl who will love the gospel, even sacrifice for it.

He blessed her to be a light to others, to be kind, and to honor womanhood all the days of her life. He blessed her to be a true and faithful daughter of God so that one day she will be prepared to make and keep sacred temple covenants.

Elizabeth, do you know if you had a blessing as a baby? Do you know someone you could ask about what was said in that blessing and who performed that ordinance? Is a blessing something you would like to have for your babies?

By the way, Elizabeth, do you know what your name means? Just for fun I thought I might send you a list of some names and their meanings. Here is a name for each letter of the alphabet:

Name	Meaning
Amy	Beloved
Brenna	Little raven
Cybill	Soothsayer
Diana	Divine
Elizabeth	Consecrated to God
Fineen	Fair offspring
Gwyneth	Fortunate, blessed
Haley	Hero
Ilyssa	Rational

Jennifer	White wave
Kelly	Of the Kelts/Celts
Laura	Laurel-crowned
Margaret	A pearl
Nola	Of noble birth
Opal	From the opal gemstone
Phyllis	A leaf
Queenie	Queen
Rebecca	To tie, to bond
Stacy	Resurrection
Trudy	Beloved
Una	Unity
Virginia	Virginal, pure
Wendy	Fair one
Xusan	(From Susan) A rose/lily
Yolanda	Violet flower
Zoe	Life

What's in a name? I have a friend named Lindsay who became engaged to a young man named Lincoln. On the day that Lindsay first told her family about their plans to be married, her mother went to her room and came back with an old journal she had kept many years ago. She opened to a page written in the springtime of the year. As she showed Lindsay and her fiancée, Lincoln, this page, they were amazed. On that special page, written several months before Lindsay was born, the entry read: "We do not know whether our new baby will be a boy or a girl. If it is a girl, we plan to name her Lindsay. If it is a boy, we will name him Lincoln." That journal entry came to be very meaningful to the young couple.

What's in a name? It is up to you what your name will mean to those who know you. I hope that you will bring great honor to your first name and your last name and to the name of Jesus Christ, which we take upon us when we are baptized. You can do this by the way

you live your life. Are you living to fulfill the finest hopes and dreams of those who chose it for you? Think of those who have loved you, guided you, walked beside you, and given you your special name. How have they helped you bring honor to your name? Are you living so that others will call your name blessed because of your goodness? Write to me about your name. Tell me why you like it (if you do).

I'll be waiting to hear from you! With great expectations,

Your friend

chapter four

Promises to Keep

"And miles to go before I sleep"

Dear Elizabeth,

I wish you could meet Whitney. She is a darling girl who is thirteen and was just baptized. I was there for her baptism and thought you might like to hear about her story.

It was a magical moment as I looked around the room at all the people there for Whitney's baptism. I spotted a girls' soccer team there. They were sitting together in their Sunday best and took up a whole row. They had been there for each other many times. That's the way it is with teams, and this team was one of the best in soccer—and in life. Each girl had set a good example for Whitney, standing as a witness of goodness at all times, in all things, and in all places, even on the playing field. Whitney had always liked being part of that. It felt good.

Then one day a tragedy had come to the family of a team member

who was Whitney's best friend. Her name was also Elizabeth. Elizabeth's older brother Mike and his wife, Natalie, had been driving home from her dance review. Their little boys, two-year-old MJ and little baby Matthew, four months old, had been sleeping soundly, all snuggled up in their car seats, when suddenly a car driven by a drunk driver had slammed into them, killing baby Matthew.

It was a stunning tragedy! One moment everyone was content and everything was happy, the next moment everything was ruined. Everyone was hurt; and saddest of all, their little baby boy with fat cheeks and sparkling eyes was gone. He was hurt so badly he couldn't live. Everybody was so sad. The extended family and friends gathered to show love and to cry together, Whitney and her soccer team included. Baby Matthew mattered to them.

The whole tragedy caused Whitney to ask some hard questions about the purpose of life and where we go after death. She wondered, *Where is baby Matthew? Is death the end? Matthew's parents say they will be with him again. How is that possible?* You see, Whitney wasn't a member of our Church and hadn't been taught about the important principles of immortality and eternal life.

Fortunately, Whitney's friends and their parents had answers for all of her hard questions. And they soon came to *her* with a question, "Would you like to learn more about your Heavenly Father's plan?" Whitney said yes, and the missionaries began to teach her. Her tender heart was touched; her questions had logical answers. She learned that baby Matthew's spirit is still living, that it was separated from his body at the time of death, and is now in heaven with Heavenly Father. She learned that his spirit and body will be reunited when he is resurrected and that one of the reasons Jesus Christ died was to make it possible for us to live again after death, all of us, including little Matthew.

Matthew and his parents and brother, MJ, are an eternal family because the parents, Mike and Natalie, were married not just "till death do you part" but for eternity in the holy temple of God. They know that their family will be forever. They will all be together again

after this life. One day, they will have the opportunity to raise Matthew to maturity. It is a beautiful and loving plan that our Savior, the Lord Jesus Christ, has made possible for us to enjoy.

Whitney gained a testimony of these truths and the other important gospel principles taught by the missionaries. She wanted to become a member of our Church and learn more about the plan of our Heavenly Father for His children. And so, on a beautiful fall day, Whitney entered the waters of baptism. Her soccer coach, who held the priesthood, baptized her. Her coach was baby Matthew's uncle.

At her baptism, Whitney made promises to Heavenly Father about how she would live her life. So did you. At baptism you promised to stand as a witness, or example, of Him at all times, in all things, and in all places. You promised to be more like Jesus Christ. When you keep that kind of promise it will help you become a finer young woman. You remember that promise, or covenant, each week as you partake of the sacrament. You promise once again, as you drink the water and eat the bread, that you will always remember the Savior and live to keep His spirit with you.

I hope that your own remembering brings you an increased desire to be all that you can be. And I hope you never forget that you have some sacred promises to keep.

I like what the poet Robert Frost wrote about keeping promises:

Stopping by Woods on a Snowy Evening

Whose woods these are I think I know.
His house is in the village though;
He will not see me stopping here
To watch his woods fill up with snow.

My little horse must think it queer
To stop without a farmhouse near
Between the woods and frozen lake
The darkest evening of the year.

He gives his harness bells a shake
To ask if there is some mistake.
The only other sound's the sweep
Of easy wind and downy flake.

The woods are lovely, dark and deep.
But I have promises to keep,
And miles to go before I sleep,
And miles to go before I sleep.[1]

Whitney's baptism and yours were just the start of an amazing journey, and you too have "miles to go before you sleep."

Do you remember your baptism? Were you baptized at the age of eight or were you older, like Whitney? Have you thought about the person who baptized you? Have you thought about some of the promises you made when you were baptized? Have you given some thought to why you needed to be baptized? Do you realize that it is the first step in the plan of Heavenly Father, the first step back to heaven? Baptism opens the gate. I'd love to have you share with me what you remember of your sacred baptism day.

Keep remembering,

I have promises to keep,
And miles to go before I sleep,
And miles to go before I sleep.

In the Company of the Comforter

The Holy Ghost shall teach you all things

Dear Elizabeth,

That was a great letter about the day of your baptism! I hope you will save those memories to share with your own children one day.

As my friend Whitney became a member of The Church of Jesus Christ of Latter-day Saints, she joined a sisterhood of more than half a million teenage girls all over the world—from France to Russia and from Africa to Australia. On that special day after her baptism, she stood with her friends, their faces glowing, their eyes bright, and their smiles sincere, to repeat these words they had learned by heart: "We are daughters of our Heavenly Father who loves us." Whitney, her friends, and you, Elizabeth, really are remarkable, precious daughters of Heavenly Father, who loves you so much that He doesn't want to leave you alone in your journey through life. The Savior promised His apostles, "I will not leave you comfortless: I will come to you" (John

14:18). He then gave them the priceless gift of the Holy Ghost. The Lord has given you the same gift, and He makes the same promise to you. Always try to live so that you can be in the company of the Comforter, the Holy Ghost.

By using this excellent gift, you will be guided in your daily life, you will gain a testimony of the gospel, and you will receive comfort.

When you received the gift of the Holy Ghost, it was as if your Father in Heaven Himself had sent you a gift to celebrate your baptism! Those who hold the holy Melchizedek Priesthood laid their hands on your head, with authority from God, to give you this wonderful gift. Heavenly Father wanted you to accept it, to *receive* it, as is stated in the confirmation prayer.

Parley P. Pratt, who served as a member of the Quorum of the Twelve Apostles in the early days of the Church, explained some of the things the Holy Ghost can do for us: "The gift of the Holy Spirit . . . inspires virtue, kindness, goodness, tenderness, gentleness and charity. It develops beauty of person, form and features. It tends to health, vigor, animation and social feeling. It develops and invigorates all the faculties of the physical and intellectual man. It strengthens, invigorates, and gives tone to the nerves. In short, it is, as it were, marrow to the bone, joy to the heart, light to the eyes, music to the ears, and life to the whole being."[1]

Elizabeth, what do you think of when you hear the word *gift*? When I think about gifts, I remember a particularly wonderful gift we received on the day my husband was inaugurated as a university president. On that memorable occasion, my parents gave us a white satin comforter mother had made for us. This elegant gift expressed their deepest love and approval. They had wanted to give us something that would also be useful. And so mother had made a quilt, a comforter, of the most precious white satin available. The design is exquisite, created by thousands of tiny, handmade, individual stitches.

Since receiving that wonderful gift, we have been wrapped in its warmth and have felt its comfort often. We have wanted to be clean

when we use that gift. It is so pure and white that it seems only right to have clean hands when we touch the gift. We have remembered Mother's love as we have examined each of the tiny stitches that made the intricate design of this treasure. We think of her with thankfulness each day as we use the white satin comforter.

In one small way, the Holy Ghost is like our quilt gift, which gives us daily comfort and reminds us of the love of our parents. Likewise, to enjoy the benefits of God's gift to us, the gift of the Holy Ghost, we must first receive it, and then use it in our lives. I hope that you have received that very precious gift from your Heavenly Father, the gift of the Holy Ghost, and put it to use in your life. Listen for the guidance of the Spirit in all you do. You will be helped in your friend-ships, your decisions, your studies, your worries and heartaches, your temptations, and all your worthy efforts and challenges. Stop and listen for impressions and direction and then follow the Spirit. Take the Spirit with you wherever you go. It can be your constant com-panion if you are worthy, if you have "clean hands, and a pure heart" (Psalm 24:4), as the scriptures say.

Elizabeth, can I share with you a sweet experience I had with the comforting power of the Holy Ghost when I was just a young girl? I had become seriously ill with a raw sore throat, an extremely high fever, a severe headache, a stiff neck, and a limp in my walk. Every muscle ached, and it was hard for me to swallow.

As the hours went by, the illness became increasingly severe. Nothing the doctor recommended helped. I remember pulling my hair as hard as I could and not even feeling it because my head ached so badly. My parents were very worried; this was their first child, and polio was raging in almost epidemic proportions in the land. It was taking the lives of many children, and those who didn't die were often left crippled. Polio was every parent's worst fear in those days.

In the middle of the night, my frightened parents decided that they needed more help. They called my grandfather to come. He and my own father administered to me using holy consecrated oil, and the power of

the holy Melchizedek Priesthood, which they held worthily. They called on God for healing, help, guidance, and comfort. They gave me a wonderful blessing. And then they took me to a doctor in another town who immediately sent us to Salt Lake City—two-and-one-half hours away—with the admonition to hurry. He was certain it was polio.

It was a cold, stormy night in October. When we finally arrived at the hospital in Salt Lake, we went through the wide hospital doors and found there were medical personnel waiting for us. They grabbed me from my parents' arms and whisked me away. Without a word of good-bye or explanation, we were separated. I was all alone, and I thought I was going to die.

Following the painful diagnostic procedures, including a spinal tap, they took me to a hospital "isolation room," where I would stay alone, with the hope that I would not infect anyone else.

I remember how very frightened I was. But I knew I was not alone because my parents had taught me to pray. I got on my knees and knelt beside the railing of the small hospital bed and asked Heavenly Father to bless me. I was crying, I remember. Heavenly Father heard my prayer even though I was only a child. He did. And He sent the Comforter to be my companion. Heavenly Father sent the Holy Ghost, and that comforting power enveloped me in quiet love.

Into my mind flooded the reminder of the blessing that had been given me by the power of the priesthood by my beloved father and grandfather. I knew that our little family and my larger extended family were on their knees pleading with heaven on my behalf. I remembered that my parents had told me my name was on the sacred prayer rolls of the temple and that there, in God's holy house, faithful Saints would unite their faith with mine in seeking a blessing of health.

I was so young and so sick, so frightened in a dark, strange hospital room, and I felt the power of the Holy Ghost. I was not alone. I was in the company of the Comforter.

The Lord promises that "because of meekness and lowliness of heart cometh the visitation of the Holy Ghost, which Comforter

filleth with hope and perfect love, which love endureth by diligence unto prayer" (Moroni 8:26).

In the long weeks that followed, I received excellent medical care and gradually began to improve and regain strength. My health began to return. We saw a miracle occurring right before our eyes. I was blessed to have a full and complete recovery. Throughout my life I have often asked, "Why me? Why did I receive such a marvelous blessing?" It has made me realize that I owe my life to the Lord. I have tried to live to show my deep gratitude.

To this day I thank God, my Heavenly Father, for blessing me with the comfort from the power of the Holy Ghost as I knelt alone in a hospital room. I thank Him for blessing me to be healed from polio. I am his indebted and very grateful daughter, trying to live worthy to have the companionship of the Holy Ghost.

Elizabeth, do you remember how you felt when hands were placed on your head following your baptism and you received the gift of the Holy Ghost? Do you know who confirmed you a member of The Church of Jesus Christ of Latter-day Saints? Have you felt the influence of the Holy Ghost in your life? You may not have had a dramatic experience like I did with polio. That was unusual. But have you had a simple, sweet experience in which you knew you felt the Spirit? Could you share it with me?

May you walk often in the company of the Comforter. May you feel that special peace and presence often, sweet friend.

With love,

Your friend

chapter six

Stand As a Witness

"At all times and in all things, and in all places"

Dear Elizabeth,

Remember our friend Whitney? I often think about her and her friends when we say in our theme we will "stand as witnesses of God at all times and in all things, and in all places." It was because Whitney's friends had stood as witnesses that we were all there on that memorable day to welcome a beautiful daughter of God into The Church of Jesus Christ of Latter-day Saints.

What does it mean to stand as a witness of God "at all times and in all things, and in all places"?

First of all, in standing as a witness at all times, we promise to love the Lord, to honor Him all the time—daytime and nighttime, summer and winter, good times and bad times—and to let that love show by the way we live. We promise to take time to thank Him, to ask for help, to seek guidance, and then to listen. And we promise to

take time for that still, small voice to whisper to us, help us, and give us courage. Let me illustrate.

Anya lives in Russia. When she was only fourteen years old, the missionaries began teaching her the gospel. One day in her school class, the teacher began saying false things about the Church and about the Book of Mormon. There were no Latter-day Saints in the school to defend it; but little Anya, who was not even a member, only an investigator of the Church, knew that what the teacher was saying was wrong. She stood up in front of the whole class and defended the Book of Mormon and the Church. What courage! She told them that what they were saying was not true and that she knew the Book of Mormon was true and if anyone wanted to know the truth for themselves, she invited them to read it like she had done. Then Anya went home and told the missionaries she was ready to be baptized.

I love Anya's courage to stand as a witness at an important time. Standing as a witness in all *things* means *all* things—big things, little things—in all conversations and jokes, in games played and books read and music listened to, in causes supported, service rendered, clothes worn, and friends made.

Kendra, another young woman I know, once told me: "I never thought that I was being an example or 'standing as a witness' when I made right choices. I was only trying to live worthy to obtain all the blessings Heavenly Father has promised me."

Standing as a witness in all things means being kind in all things, being the first to say hello, being the first to smile, being the first to make the stranger feel a part of things. It means being helpful, thinking of others' feelings, and being inclusive.

Our Heavenly Father does bless us when we show our love for Him in all things.

A really important thing for you to remember, Elizabeth, is that we say we will stand as witnesses in all *places*. This includes public places, and private places, secret places, dark places, and light places as well. It includes church, school, home, or cars, mountain places or

beach places. We need to stand as examples of worthy daughters of God in *all* places.

I first read about Shannon in the *New Era*. Her high school speech teacher had assigned a group project to the students. They were to select a scene from a play to perform for the class. One group chose a questionable scene that dealt with morality issues. The teacher allowed them to keep their selection "for the sake of art." Knowing, however, that it might be offensive, the teacher gave permission for those who felt uncomfortable to leave the room.

As the students' scene began, Shannon felt a little nervous. Several of her classmates acted a bit embarrassed, but no one left. She looked at a few of her Latter-day Saint friends, hoping one of them might do something. But none of them did. Shannon remained at her desk with her head down so no one could see her crimson cheeks. She felt very uncomfortable, but she was also afraid to leave. After all, it was art, right? Shannon said, "At this moment, the Young Women theme came into my mind: 'We will "stand as witnesses of God at all times and in all things, and in all places."' . . . Immediately, I knew what I should do. 'All places' meant everywhere, even in a classroom with my friends. Quietly, I got up and left the room. That was it. No one got up and followed me. No one applauded my valiant act. No one was converted by my example. But inside I knew I had done the right thing."[1]

I received a letter from Shannon last week. Today she is married and has two little boys. She is a Young Women leader in her ward. It is so much fun for me to keep in touch with wonderful girls and learn about "the rest of their stories." I hope we can always remain good friends, Elizabeth. I love hearing about your life and your experiences and feelings.

Well, let's get back to the subject. Did you notice something each of these young women has in common? In order to stand as a witness, each young woman exercised good judgment. Have you heard it said

of someone, "she has good judgment?" What a great compliment! Exercising good judgment is a sign of maturity and trustworthiness.

Our Heavenly Father has asked us to make judgments. The Book of Mormon tells us that "It is given unto you to judge, that ye may know good from evil; and the way to judge is as plain, that ye may know with a perfect knowledge, as the daylight is from the dark night" (Moroni 7:15). We can know clearly! How? The way to do this is laid out for us very simply in the next verse: "For every thing which [1] inviteth to do good, and [2] to persuade to believe in Christ, is sent forth by the power and gift of Christ; wherefore ye may know with a perfect knowledge it is of God."

But listen to this from verse 17: "Whatsoever thing persuadeth men to [1] do evil, and [2] believe not in Christ, and [3] deny him, and [4] serve not God, then ye may know with a perfect knowledge it is of the devil; . . . for he persuadeth no man to do good, no, not one." Remember Joseph who was sold into Egypt? Certainly he exercised good judgment when he was tempted by Potiphar's wife to become involved with her in an immoral act (Genesis 39:7–12). We read in the Bible that at this critical time in his young life, Joseph stood up and got himself out of the situation. He didn't sit around wondering what to do. He didn't linger a little longer. He *stood*, stood as a witness of righteousness at this crucial time. He exercised good judgment, and it made all the difference.

You, like Joseph, are of noble heritage. You have a royal inheritance, for you are a spirit daughter of God. You are of a chosen generation. You were chosen before this world was to come forth at this time. You were taught in a premortal world by God Himself.

President Ezra Taft Benson said something about this that I'd like to share with you. He said: "You have been born at this time for a sacred and glorious purpose. It is not by chance that you have been reserved to come to earth in this last dispensation of the fulness of times. Your birth at this particular time was foreordained in the eternities."[2]

Elizabeth, the time is here for you to stand up for what you know is right. You must judge right from wrong. You can't afford to be complacent, or go with the flow, or wonder what to do. You must decide now which path you will follow, which answer you will give. Decide well in advance, before the pressure is on, what you stand for.

If I were Satan and wanted to destroy a generation, I would aim my assault at young women. And I think this is exactly what Satan does. By doing so, he can strike two birds with one stone, so to speak. By deceiving the young women of today, he can control those of the next generation as well, for you are the ones who will nurture and teach those of future generations.

The good news, however, is that you can win any assault aimed at you! And it is not that hard. Just use good judgment! You can stand up and change the channel on the television, turn off the pornography on the computer, leave a movie theater, and rent movies that are clean and fun. Don't wear revealing clothes that are too tight, too bare, or too short. Leave them in the closet. Better still, leave them in the store. Stand up and walk away from temptation, just like Joseph did—only he didn't just walk away, he ran! You can do this too, literally and figuratively, and you will be safer, more pure, more secure.

I hope you were able to join in a special fireside for youth given by President Gordon B. Hinckley in November 2000. It was wonderful! In talking about challenges, he told us: "Of all the challenges that have been faced in the past, the ones we have today, I believe, are the most easily handled. I say that because they are manageable. They largely involve individual behavioral decisions, but those decisions can be made and followed. And when that happens, the challenge is behind us."[3]

Be cautious of those things Satan will use as he tries to disrupt God's plan for you. One thing he does is desensitize young women. He gives them a small, seemingly innocent taste of something ultimately destructive. Next time he gives a little more, and next time

even more, until soon it is time for the big whammy, which is hardly even even noticed. Nephi taught that the "devil cheateth their souls, and leadeth them away *carefully* down to hell" (2 Nephi 28:21; emphasis added). Elizabeth, don't allow yourself to be "carefully" desensitized by gradual lapses in good judgment.

As you view images, whether on TV or videos, movies or the Internet, you will see some things that are good and most probably you will have opportunity to see things that are not good. Wrong and evil will be made to appear acceptable. Don't be tricked! Simply stand up and walk away!

Dear Elizabeth, you know some things that the good people of the world don't know because you have been taught truth. You have all you need to stand strong and firm and true because you have the Lord on your side. The Savior will help you stand strong by the power of His love. He can strengthen and bless you.

The Lord still performs miracles today to bless our lives, large and small miracles. He will help you, through His holy power and His great love for you, to stand strong in the face of difficult circumstances. Certainly He can do this because He has the power to strengthen, to lift, to heal. You must simply learn to depend on Him.

I love what President Benson said about depending on the Lord: "Men and women who turn their lives over to God will discover that He can make a lot more out of their lives than they can. He will deepen their joys, expand their vision, quicken their minds, strengthen their muscles, lift their spirits, multiply their blessings, increase their opportunities, comfort their souls, raise up friends, and pour out peace. Whoever will lose his life in the service of God will find eternal life."[4]

Elizabeth, there are so many of us who care about you. Walk with us. Draw close to God. "Be thou humble; and the Lord thy God shall lead thee by the hand, and give thee answer to thy prayers" (D&C 112:10). Put your hand in His, and He will lead and guide you in peace.

I think it is truly remarkable that the world still remembers that little baby boy born in Bethlehem so long ago who grew in wisdom and stature. He was perfect. He lived a life that we still try to follow. He showed us the way. He taught truths we still try to live. They are as true today as they were then, for truth never changes.

He willingly suffered for our sins because He loved us so completely. He gave us the right to repent. And He gave His life that we might be resurrected and live again after death.

Elizabeth, when you think of the magnificence of His gift to you, can you think of some things you could do for Him to show your love and gratitude? Maybe you could write down some of the ways that you try to show your love for Him as you "stand as a witness" in your daily life.

With admiration and love,

Your friend

_____

_____

_____

_____

_____

_____

chapter seven

You Are Loved

"we are daughters of our Heavenly Father who loves us"

Dear Elizabeth,

I was thinking about you today and wondered if you know how much you are loved. I guess that was because of my visit with a young woman recently who felt so unloved that she had done some very foolish things. When I asked her if she prayed, she said she sometimes did. I asked her if she read the scriptures every day. She said she used to but was now reading a good novel about the Church by a popular author. And she also told me that she couldn't feel Heavenly Father's love. I told her about Fairy May.

I know of a play where one of the characters has the enchanting name of Fairy May. At one point in the play, Fairy May complains: "No one has told me they love me this live long day." Someone replies, "Oh, yes they have!" Fairy May says, "No they haven't! I've been listening and no one has told me they love me." Another

character says, "Fairy May, remember when I said, 'take an umbrella, it's raining?' That was one way of saying I love you and I don't want you to get wet in the rain so take an umbrella! Remember when someone else said, 'Wear a sweater, it's cold?' That was a way of saying I care about you, I love you, and don't want you to get cold." Fairy May listened, and gradually she began to understand that indeed she was loved and that love had been expressed to her in many different ways that day and every day.[1]

I sometimes wonder how many of us suffer from what we could call the Fairy May Syndrome? How many of us don't feel loved? As I read letters from young women, I become sad when I find there are girls who don't feel loved. These young girls are mistaken. There is always One who loves you very, very dearly, more than can be imagined.

The Lord tells us of His love when He teaches us how to return to Him. He loves us so very much that He wants us to come back to heaven! The first step on the path homeward is to make baptismal covenants. Allowing us to take the sacrament each week is one way He reminds us of His great love and His longing for our return home. The sacrament is a very real and physical way to remind us of His love for us.

That is only the beginning. Heavenly Father has also given each of us unique gifts. Oh, dear Elizabeth, how He loves you!

A little two-year-old boy I know was busy coloring on a paper when someone complimented him by saying, "Jackson, what beautiful big brown eyes you have! Where did you get those eyes?" Little Jackson replied, "Baby Gap" (the name of a children's clothing store).

While Jackson's reply was cute and funny, he will soon learn that Heavenly Father gave him his beautiful brown eyes and his cute dimple and his thick blonde hair. He will come to know that Heavenly Father wants him to be happy here on earth and to be successful here in his earthly mission so that he can return home.

Heavenly Father has, in fact, given all of us everything we need to do just that.

Consider the gifts Heavenly Father has given you, Elizabeth. Do you ever stop to count all those gifts, your blessings? All that we have was given by One who loves us more than we can understand. I like this poem because it makes it clear how blessed we are without even knowing it.

The World Is Mine!

Today upon a bus I saw a lovely maid with golden hair;
I envied her—she seemed so gay—
    and wished I were as fair.
When suddenly she rose to leave,
    I saw her hobble down the aisle;
She had one foot and wore a crutch,
    but as she passed, a smile.
Oh, God, forgive me when I whine.
I have two feet; the world is mine!

And then I stopped to buy some sweets.
The lad that sold them had such charm.
I talked with him, he said to me,
"It's nice to talk with folks like you.
You see," he said, "I'm blind."
Oh, God, forgive me when I whine.
I have two eyes; the world is mine!

Then walking down the street,
I saw a child with eyes of blue.
He stood and watched the others play;
It seemed he knew not what to do.
I stopped for a moment, then I said,
"Why don't you join the others, dear?"
He looked ahead without a word,

And then I knew he could not hear.
Oh, God, forgive me when I whine.
I have two ears; the world is mine!

With feet to take me where I'd go,
With eyes to see the sunset's glow,
With ears to hear what I would know,
Oh, God, forgive me when I whine.
I'm blessed, indeed! The world is mine![2]

Food for thought, isn't it?

King Benjamin, in the Book of Mormon, lists some of the ways Heavenly Father shows His love for us, reminding us that (1) God created us; (2) He preserves us from day to day; (3) He lends us our very breath so that we can move about; and (4) He supports us from one moment to the next. Then, when we keep His commandments, (5) God prospers us. (Mosiah 2:21–22).

Other scriptures teach us that "We love him, because he first loved us" (1 John 4:19).

As you can tell, Elizabeth, I love poems . . . they say it so well! This is a classic about love written by the romantic poet, Elizabeth Barrett Browning (there's that name again—feeling famous?):

How do I love thee? Let me count the ways.
I love thee to the depth and breadth and height
My soul can reach, when feeling out of sight
For the ends of Being and Ideal Grace.
I love thee to the level of everyday's
Most quiet need, by sun and candle-light.
I love thee freely, as men strive for Right;
I love thee purely, as they turn from Praise.
I love thee with the passion put to use
In my old griefs, and with my childhood's faith.
I love thee with a love I seemed to lose

With my lost saints—I love thee with the breath,
Smiles, tears, of all my life!—and, if God choose,
I shall but love thee better after death.[3]

You could follow the example of the poets and even King Benjamin and count all the ways our Heavenly Father loves you. The list could become very lengthy. Elizabeth, how long is your list? I'd love to have you share with me some of the ways you know that you are loved. You could add to that list each day in your journal.

Write soon. And please know that I love you too!

Counting all "the ways," I remain,

Your friend

_____

_____

_____

_____

_____

_____

_____

chapter eight

Your Gift to Him

make it a masterpiece!

Dear Liz,

Have you ever been called Liz? Is it okay if I use that nickname?
Do you like it?

I loved reading your expressions of love for your Heavenly Father,
who has given you so much. You will come to know that an important way to show our Heavenly Father that we love Him is to make
our life a glorious gift to Him.

I'm sure you've heard the saying, "Your life is God's gift to you.
What you make of your life is your gift to God." Each of us wants to
give the very finest gift possible to God. I know that you do too. So
each day, each step along the way, try to make your life something
very special.

We have talked about what your Heavenly Father has so gener-
ously given you. Now it is time to focus on your part of the plan. How

are you developing and using the gifts and talents He has given you? Are you preparing to contribute in a valuable way throughout your life?

Can you imagine in your mind's eye what wonderful things you could accomplish in your life as you prepare your "gift"? I have a vision of what the future could hold for you and your friends. Dream with me.

I can see girls who will grow to become women who will create homes in the neighborhoods of the world, who will nurture future generations, who will combat evil, who will work to right wrongs, who will contribute love and joy and laughter to the world, who will create beauty and peace. You will calm fears and build faith. You could be a woman who will love and strengthen and empower a husband, who will help build an eternal family. You may face fear and disappointment, even betrayal, but can go on to lift and inspire. You could be a woman who will create works of art and literature, who will provide the very basics of shelter, sustenance, and nurture. The products of your mind could open new vistas for mankind. You and your friends will be women who will sweep a floor, iron a shirt, stir the soup, wipe a nose, bandage a cut, cure a disease.

Liz, you are preparing for your future by learning and practicing on your family and friends today. Can you imagine yourself as a mother? Picture yourself in ten years. What will you be doing? Will you be getting an education or learning a useful skill? What will you be like? In your mind's eye, do you see yourself as a nurturer of precious sons and daughters of Heavenly Father? You can practice now by being loving and gentle to little children and by saying the kindest things in the kindest way in your own home. Do you picture yourself as a mother who could help her children with learning math or science or history?

I recently read the obituary of a mother who inspired her family. The newspaper read: "Mrs. Cole sparked a thirst for knowledge in her children. She was the only mother on the block to provide ether-anesthetized bullfrogs to teach her sons amphibian anatomy. When her young sons brought home dead gophers, she cheerfully surrendered

her pressure cooker to boil off the meat and assemble skeletons. When living in Los Angeles, she was a volunteer at the Metabolic Research Unit at UCLA. Her role was to set up from scratch a serum calcium assay for use in myeloma research. Among her choicest memories were the times that the medical staff would slip over from the UCLA Hospital with a sample of blood and ask her to give them the 'real' serum calcium level.

"She taught her sons to pray, to make cinnamon rolls, and to hum Brahms' lullaby. She fulfilled many callings in The Church of Jesus Christ of Latter-day Saints which brought her joy."[1]

Many people are indebted to this great woman, for a son she taught to love science, grew up to be a wonderful doctor who has solved medical problems for many grateful patients.

Like this woman, the time may come in your life, Elizabeth, when you will be called upon to provide for yourself and, possibly, your family. That could happen for numerous reasons. With that in mind, guess what you'd better do at school? Work hard! Education is the best insurance policy available.

Do you want to have beauty and music and refinement in your home? Today you can begin developing your artistic and musical talents for the sake of your future home and family. Do you want to have peace and order in your home? Then today be the peacemaker; help keep your home clean and orderly, help with the laundry.

Can you imagine your future family sitting around a table laughing and sharing ideas and enjoying the delicious, nutritious food that you have prepared with love? If you can, it looks like you'll have to learn to cook! Help prepare the meals. Collect recipes from your mother and your grandmother and from your friends' moms. Learn how to make strudel, or stew, or pasta—family favorites, whatever they are.

I see in you a young woman who is getting an education, who is developing talents and skills, and who is preparing to bless others through that preparation. Please, for yourself and for your future

family, choose a fine education and the best preparation. Be qualified. Be well rounded. Work hard. In you, I see a girl who looks forward to establishing a home of love, a home of happiness and accomplishment, a home of order, a home of faith.

I see in you and your friends young women who understand that the things you do today will make you the kind of strong, faithful women that the Lord needs to bless His children. You want to teach your families of Heavenly Father and His ways, and you know how and where to go for that preparation—scripture study, Church meetings, prayer, seminary, family home evening.

Because we were sent here to earth to be tested and to prove ourselves, there may be some things in life that won't turn out exactly as we have dreamed. That's the way with earthly life. But remember this, when you work hard and prepare yourself to make contributions, when you keep the covenants you made at baptism and others you will make later on in the temple, you can meet any of the challenges of life with faith and hope and courage!

As part of His plan, Heavenly Father provided a Savior who will help us in this life. The Savior said, "This is my work and my glory—to bring to pass the immortality and eternal life of man" (Moses 1:39). Because of Him we can correct mistakes we make in life, be forgiven, and start fresh. Because of Him we can return to heaven one day. He loves you. He wants you to be successful! And He will help you succeed in your life's mission.

Here is a little tip: as you grow, observe the faithful women you admire and then adopt into your own life the qualities that make them successful and happy daughters of God. He will help you do that because He wants you to be the best you can be!

In preparation for your future, may I invite you to do something today? Would you please write all about the kind of woman you would like to become? Then will you work toward making the dream of your future become a reality in your life? In this way, you will begin to develop your wonderful gift for Heavenly Father, the gift you will

bring with you when you return to Him—your best self. You can make it a masterpiece!

Can't wait to hear from you.

With love,

Your friend

_____

_____

_____

_____

_____

_____

_____

_____

_____

_____

_____

chapter nine

It Takes Courage

He shall prepare a way

Dear Elizabeth,

In recent letters, you have asked some very insightful questions about courage. I understand how much courage it takes to live in the right way. Sometimes it takes courage to follow a prompting.

Do you remember reading about when valiant Nephi went to get the brass plates from Laban? Have you read about the experience in the beginning pages of the Book of Mormon? Remember what happened? He and his brothers went to do something that was hard to do and they didn't know how they were going to accomplish it, but Nephi said, "I will go and do the things which the Lord hath commanded, for I know that the Lord giveth no commandments unto the children of men, save he shall prepare a way for them that they may accomplish the thing which he commandeth them" (1 Nephi 3:7). What an exciting story comes from Nephi's courage to accomplish his

mission and get the brass plates! If you haven't read it lately, would you please read it in 1 Nephi chapters 3 and 4? Apply the principles it teaches to your own life. Even though the Lord hasn't asked you to get the brass plates, He has asked you to stand as an example to the world, and youth everywhere are doing it.

Do you remember the Russian girl, Anya, I wrote to you about? She stood up for the Book of Mormon and the Church in one of her school classes. When I was in Russia, I learned that Anya had ridden on a train for twelve hours just to attend the meeting where I spoke. It was a small meeting compared to many that I have spoken at in the United States, but the few members who were there were happy, valiant souls. After the third hour ended, Anya and three other girls got back on the train and rode twelve hours home. When I think of Anya I think of the scripture, "Be not weary in well-doing, for ye are laying the foundation of a great work. And out of small things proceedeth that which is great" (D&C 64:33).

Anya has found great joy in living the gospel. Soon after she made her courageous stand in defense of the Book of Mormon, her mother recognized the source of Anya's joy and she too joined the Church. Just a few months ago I received word that her older brother, a student in dental school who said he would never join the Church, has just been baptized. Their little brother wants to become a member as well and will when he is old enough. Now they have only their father left outside the Church. I have a feeling that if this family faithfully lives the gospel, its light will continue to radiate in their lives, and their father, whom they all love so much, will surely join them as a member of the Church.

I know another young woman who lives in the Philippines who is coming closer to the Savior. She is the only member of the Church in her family. I will call her Maria. Every Sunday she walks many miles across a vast, deep field and through a wide river to get to church. But she doesn't come alone, she brings her little brother with her. Because he is so small, she carries him on her back much of the

way; she wants him to learn the gospel and love it and live it as she does.

When Nephi was faced with how to get across the water—a vast ocean, much greater than the river my friend in the Philippines crossed—he was commanded by the Lord to build a ship. His older brothers made fun of him and laughed and mocked him for trying. But once again, Nephi was filled with courage. This courage came by the power of God, who loved His faithful son. Nephi went ahead and built a ship that took his family to the promised land (1 Nephi 17, 18). Maria, this precious young woman who carries her brother to church, has surely received courage and faith from the same source Nephi used.

Dear, wonderful, remarkable young friend, I am honored to know you. For I know that you are full of greatness and courage, much like that of Nephi and Anya and Maria. You are like a hero to me. Heavenly Father loves you very much.

Remember when I told you that even before you were born you received your first lessons in the world of spirits and were prepared to come forth at this time in the history of the world (D&C 138:56)? You were born to womanhood, and that is a special privilege. You can't even imagine how much Heavenly Father loves you and wants to see you succeed in your life. He wants to see you stay morally pure and clean and prepare yourself to make sacred temple covenants. He wants to see you establish a home which you will fill with beauty and love and goodness. A home of prayer, a home of order, a home of learning and accomplishment. He wants you to live to inspire the young men who are your friends, and nurture and teach the children of future generations. He wants you to fill your life with so much goodness and truth that others will be attracted to it and want to embrace it like Anya's family did.

Being completely active in Church programs will strengthen your testimony and help you become a better person. For example, I know of a young woman who lives in the United States. She was working

with the Personal Progress program and, as one of her goals, wrote that she wanted to live worthy to be married for time and all eternity in the holy temple of God. Then, as we do in the Personal Progress program, she talked with her mother about her goal, even though her mother was not active in the Church. Susan's mom didn't say very much to her, but in her heart she too set a goal. The goal was that she, herself, would work to be married in the temple and be sealed for time and all eternity to her family. There was one major problem (besides her inactivity). The problem was that her husband, Susan's father, wasn't a member of the Church. One day, when the time was right, Heavenly Father gave Susan's mom the courage to tell her husband about their daughter's goal of a temple marriage and about her own goal. Do you know what happened? The father said, "Well, if that's the case, I guess we'd better invite the missionaries over so I can find out what this church is all about!"

The rest of the story is that Susan's father was baptized and her parents were sealed in the temple, with their children. What a miracle! And all because of the courage of a great teenage girl.

Elizabeth, you are the future of the kingdom of God. President Hinckley has said that you are part of a royal generation. You are born to royalty because you are a child of a King, the Lord God, King of Heaven and Earth.

Sister Carol B. Thomas, a counselor in the Young Women general presidency, spoke recently about your own nobility. She said: "A story is told of the son of King Louis XVI of France. As a young man, he was kidnapped by evil men when they dethroned the king. For six months he was exposed to every filthy and vile thing that life had to offer, yet he never buckled under the pressure. This puzzled his captors, and they asked him why he had such great moral strength. His reply was simple: 'I cannot do what you ask, for I was born to be a king.' . . . You were born to be daughters of a King. By being baptized, you have been promised the blessings of royalty as you sanctify yourselves and become holy."[1]

So, how do you do it? How can you become more holy and claim your royal heritage? Christ has said, "Follow me, and do the things which ye have seen me do" (2 Nephi 31:12).

The Lord will help you, just as He did Nephi. He will prepare the way. He did for Nephi. But Nephi had to go and do . . . do something. And as he went, the Lord showed him the way to go and what to do. Each step of the way, he was helped and guided. He had opposition. He didn't know what to do next sometimes. He tried one thing and it didn't work so he tried again. Did his brothers want to help him? No! Nephi had to have great courage. There is a Primary song about the courage of Nephi, and I'd like to share part of it with you. Do you remember it from your Primary days?

> The Lord gives us commandments and asks us to obey.
> Sometimes I am tempted to choose another way.
> When I'm discouraged, and think I cannot try,
> I will be courageous, and I will reply:
> "I will go; I will do the thing the Lord commands.
> I know the Lord provides a way; he wants me to obey."[2]

The story of Nephi is a great scripture story. But that is a story about a young man who lived thousands of years ago. What about today? What about the things that are going on here in your life?

You are a teenager and a member of the Church. Is it easy to live the gospel when sometimes you are the only one trying? Is it easy to be the only member of the Church in the family? Is it easy to dress modestly when the styles aren't modest? Is it easy to keep your behavior clean and pure when the rest of the world doesn't believe in that kind of lifestyle? During your teen years, Heavenly Father will ask you to make important decisions—vital choices. You can use the formulas given in the Book of Mormon, formulas that Nephi and other righteous men and women followed. Read Moroni 7 again.

I see you saying no to temptation and worldly ways. I believe you have that kind of courage. It's not easy, but it is right. It takes courage

to be different. You can be different in good ways. And that is appealing to good people. As you are kind and friendly to others and set a great example, you will attract them to you. Not because they are attracted by your body, but because they are attracted to your great spirit. You can choose clothes that aren't too short or too tight, tops that are not bare and revealing, and you will be blessed with courage when you need it. Just like Anya in Russia, and Maria in the Philippines, and Susan in the United States.

It is my prayer, dear, precious Elizabeth, that you will have the courage you need "at all times and in all things, and in all places." Have you had to have courage at home, at school, with friends, with family, and in the neighborhood? Have you used courage when choosing your clothes and your language and your behavior with boys? I'd love to have you share some of those experiences with me.

Heavenly Father will prepare a way for you. This is His promise. Of this I testify. You belong to the true Church directed by Him through a prophet. Follow the prophet. Stay close to the Church. May the Lord bless you with courage, my precious friend. You can do it!

Your friend

chapter ten

To You We Throw the Torch

" . . . be yours to hold it high"

Dear Elizabeth,

I have always remembered my visit to a cemetery in England many years ago. Buried in this cemetery were thousands of young men from another country who had given their lives on foreign soil in defense of freedom. These young soldiers were really the best blood of their generation, and it was tragic that they had been claimed by the horrors of war. As we stood looking out over the acres of green grass covered by thousands of white crosses marking the graves, our attention was drawn to the flag flying over this sacred spot. At the base of the flagpole these words were inscribed: "To you from failing hands we throw the torch; be yours to hold it high."[1]

The torch—a symbol of courage and of faith. The torch was passed from these brave soldiers to those able to live and carry on.

Each of us has been handed a torch—a symbolic torch—a gospel

torch, which can light the path for others. The Lord is counting on you to help Him, Elizabeth. Young women have a torch as our logo. We can hold that "torch" high by our exemplary living and by sharing gospel truths.

As I stood there that day reading those impressive words, "To you from failing hands we throw the torch, be yours to hold it high," my mind went to the great prophet Moroni. I could just picture him writing his last words on the plates and then burying them up, knowing that one day, in the due time of the Lord, they would be brought forth to bless God's children, like a torch to light the way. Listen to his lonely and poignant words as he wrote on the sacred and precious records of his fathers for the last time:

"Behold I, Moroni, do finish the record of my father, Mormon. Behold, I have but few things to write, which things I have been commanded by my father.

"And now it came to pass that after the great and tremendous battle at Cumorah, behold, the Nephites who had escaped into the country southward were hunted by the Lamanites, until they were all destroyed.

"And my father also was killed by them, and I even remain alone to write the sad tale of the destruction of my people. But behold, they are gone, and I fulfil the commandment of my father. And whether they will slay me, I know not.

"Therefore I will write and hide up the records in the earth; and whither I go it mattereth not" (Mormon 8:1–4).

Doesn't that sound to you a little bit like, "To you from failing hands I throw the torch?"

Now listen to the next part, because he prophesied that this great sacred record that was hidden up would again come forth. He says, "And blessed be he that shall bring this light to light; for it shall be brought out of darkness unto light, according to the word of God; yea, it shall be brought out of the earth, and it shall shine forth out of

darkness, and come unto the knowledge of the people; and it shall be done by the power of God" (Mormon 8:16).

That is the part about "Be yours to hold it high." This great record, the Book of Mormon, was preserved and brought forth by the power of a loving Father in Heaven to bless and guide the lives of His children in these latter days. It is like a torch. You and I have been called to share it with others, to hold its teachings out for others to see. The Book of Mormon has the power to change lives, to give direction, to inspire, to teach, to build faith. Its words shed light on my understanding of the gospel every time I read from its pages. How grateful I am for it!

As you read and study the gospel and the Book of Mormon, you will see the flame of your torch growing brighter. As you determine to live the commandments of God with exactness and honor, you will be a guide and a light to others. Your parents and friends will be blessed because of your good example. They will sense a special spirit and light that you will radiate. The spirit will work through you to touch hearts. Your understanding will deepen and increase because your spirit will be receptive.

Let me share with you an example of the importance of one little light in the darkness. It was just a few days before Christmas, and Steve and I were a newly married couple, expecting our first child, and traveling home for the Christmas holidays. It was a long trip (forty-two hours driving) from Boston to home, but we were eager, especially me, to come home for Christmas. We filled the car with friends who would help pay for the gas and take turns driving, and then we headed for home. Oh, there truly is no place like home for the holidays, and our spirits were high in anticipation of being reunited with loved ones again! We were about two thirds of the way home, going through the plains of Nebraska, when we drove into a blinding blizzard of snow blowing and billowing and growing deeper and deeper on the highway with each passing moment. The night was pure black, and the storm was absolutely fierce. Before long we were

trying to plow through at least a foot of snow as we crept along the freeway. We couldn't see the lines of the road and couldn't see where we were going. This was literally a blinding snowstorm. Suddenly in front of us there appeared a huge semi-truck going slowly and steadily ahead. We could barely make out his small red taillights, but seeing them gave us hope. My husband, who was the driver, fixed his eyes on the small lights from the truck and then we drove along in the tracks he made through the deepening snow. Our panic subsided somewhat with that guide up ahead because he sat up higher in his rig and could perhaps have a better view, and surely he was equipped with a CB radio whereby he could get some help from others who were ahead of us down the road.

With prayers on our lips and white-knuckled hands holding on, we followed our unsuspecting leader through the storm. We passed many cars off both sides of the road, but we kept moving slowly forward. Before long we could sense that the semi was slowing down and pulling off the roadway. We followed him and soon found ourselves safely in the parking lot of what looked to be an overcrowded motel. We were to a place of refuge and we were so very, very grateful. We all hurried inside and got the last room in the place. We hurried to the truck driver and thanked him profusely for leading us to safety.

Dear friend, there will be times in life when you will feel that you are in a blizzard. It won't be a snowstorm like we experienced, but it will be a storm even more dangerous to your soul. You will be looking for a way to safety. The Savior can help you find the way through the blizzards in your life. He has had experience with trials in this life; He knows the route, He has traveled it Himself. He sits up in a higher place than we do and has a clear view of the road ahead. He will communicate with us if we tune in to His frequency. We are all equipped with the power of prayer whereby we can communicate with Him and receive His guidance. He has had more experience than we have had. He is ahead of us on the road. He is our eternal guide and guardian. The light from the gospel truths He taught will

guide you to safety within the kingdom of God. How very much better that will be than the overcrowded motel where we found refuge!

Elizabeth, as you travel through your life, perhaps there will be someone following your light; maybe it will be one of your loved ones, a family member. No one can tell whose life or how many lives you will bless. Perhaps you will find that you are an answer to someone's prayer. Will your torch be burning bright enough for that person to see your light?

Let me share with you the story about Mettie Marie Kjar, who lived in Norway. She dreamed one night about a new religion, and it all seemed so real that she awakened her husband and told him about it. She arose from her bed and went to tell her brother about it. She said, "We will join that church." Her brother seemed a bit upset about it.

Some time later, early one morning, as her husband was making the fire, two young Mormon missionaries knocked on their door. They came in and talked to him and gave him a Book of Mormon.

Mettie Marie's husband took the book into the bedroom and told her that here was the new religion she had dreamed about. As they were taught by the missionaries and learned more about the gospel, they were both greatly impressed and felt that it was the right church. The light of Christ touched their hearts, and soon a testimony of Jesus Christ burned so strongly in their souls that they could not deny the truthfulness of it. They were baptized at great personal sacrifice. So were her brother and his family. I am eternally and forever grateful for those two missionaries, for Mettie Marie and her husband, Lars Christian Kjar, are my great-great-grandparents. The light that they followed all those years ago still burns brightly in my heart and soul. And the torch that was kindled in Norway has continued to burn from one generation to the next, being carried by their posterity to nearly every corner of the earth. We cannot count the lives that have been affected, the other torches that have been lit from the first contact of those faithful missionaries on a cold, early winter morning far, far from home.

My dear friend, on a morning when it is hard to arise early enough for your morning prayer, on a warm summer evening when friends tempt you to do something you know is wrong, after a discouraging day at school, will you pause for just a moment and listen to someone, maybe even Moroni, whispering to you down from the ages: "To you from failing hands we throw the torch; be yours to hold it high"?

And then will you determine to study the words of the prophets just a little harder, to pray a little longer, to be a little more steady, to hold your torch just a little higher? After all, someone may be trying to follow your light. I pray that you will come to know the literal meaning of the grand scripture in 1 Nephi 17:13: "And I will also be your light in the wilderness; and I will prepare the way before you, if it so be that ye shall keep my commandments; wherefore, inasmuch as ye shall keep my commandments ye shall be led towards the promised land; and ye shall know that it is by me that ye are led."

Have you had the opportunity to hold a torch to light the way a little better for another—a friend or a family member? Or has someone done that for you? I would love to have you share such an experience with me!

Elizabeth, I bear a testimony that is sacred and dear to me, that the Lord is our light, our salvation, and that only through Him and by Him can we come home again to live with our Father in Heaven.

Sincerely,

chapter eleven

Follow the Light

"The Lord is my light"

Dear Elizabeth,

Have you ever stumbled around in the dark and stubbed your toe and said, "Ouch, that hurts!"? If the lights went out in your room tonight, would you be frightened or confused? Darkness can be hazardous to our health—our physical and spiritual health! It is a great blessing to have light in our lives—light that helps us see things as they really are; light that illuminates our understanding; light we can follow with confidence and perfect trust.

One young woman wrote to me about the light that illuminated the road she was on. She said, "I was with a group of my friends watching a video. It was one I knew I shouldn't be sitting through. The Spirit prompted me to leave. I was able to listen and get up and leave. I felt the Spirit so strong. I know it was because of the choice I made."[1] She followed the light to safety.

That same light showed two teenage sisters the way to go on a very frightening day in 1833. An angry mob stormed through the quiet streets of Independence, Missouri, where fifteen-year-old Mary Elizabeth Rollins and her thirteen-year-old sister Caroline lived. The terrifying mob destroyed property, burning and rioting in the streets. Some of the mobsters broke into Brother William Phelps's home, where the printing press was located. He had been printing revelations received by the Prophet Joseph Smith. They tore apart the printing press and threw it into the street. They carried the priceless, printed pages out of the building, throwing them in a pile in the yard to burn.

Mary Elizabeth and her sister Caroline were hiding behind a fence, trembling as they watched the destruction. Mary knew full well the danger of angry mobs, but in spite of that, she felt the urgency to save those precious pages. The two teenage sisters ran out to the street, grabbed arms full of the scriptures, and fled. Some of the mob saw this and ordered them to stop as they chased after the courageous sisters. The girls ran into a large cornfield where they fell breathless to the ground. Between the rows of corn they laid the copies of the revelations on the ground and then spread themselves over the pages. The men were relentless in their search for the girls among the tall cornstalks, coming very near at times, but they never were able to find the girls and eventually they gave up and left to finish their destruction in the town. We have a sculpture of those sisters in the Young Women office to remind us of the courage of young women then and now. Next time you visit our office in Salt Lake City, I hope you will take time to look at the sculpture we have there, which depicts those two courageous teenage girls.

In your own life, evil may—at first—not be as frightening as those mobs of men with painted faces, carrying torches of fire and tar and feathers to torture their victims with; but evil will destroy you just as surely as the raging mobs in Nauvoo sought to destroy the early Saints.

Looking at pornography opens the door to the destroyer of your soul. When an unmarried person touches the private, sacred parts of

another person's body to whom they are not married, they are driving with one wheel off the edge of the cliff, ready to plummet into a world of evil. When youth give in to the invitation, the temptation to experiment with beer, alcohol, marijuana, or other illicit drugs, they allow a member of Satan's mob to influence them.

Dear friend, please don't say, "But I'm too weak," if these situations arise. You are not too weak! You can do it! You have God and the angels of heaven on your side. The Lord tells His missionaries: "I will be on your right hand and on your left, and my Spirit shall be in your hearts, and mine angels round about you, to bear you up" (D&C 84:88). This is consistent with what He tells His children about His interest in helping them fulfill their life's mission.

The light of the Lord showed Mary Elizabeth and Caroline what to do and where to go for safety. That same light shines for you. It can keep you safe, just as it did them.

Let me tell you the story of another great pioneer, Jane Allgood Bailey. Jane wasn't about to give up the light of her new religion. She would not be defeated by the cold, starvation, and sickness on the plains of Wyoming. She grasped hands with other women to wade through icy streams. They came out on the other side with their clothes frozen to them, but they carried on. On the trek, her eighteen-year-old son Langley became ill and was so weak that he had to be pushed on the handcart much of the way. One morning he rose from his bed on the cart, which had frozen canvas for bedding, and went ahead of the company and lay down under a sagebrush to die, feeling that he was too much of a burden. When his faithful mother found him, she scolded him and told him, "Get on the cart. I'll help you, but you're not giving up!" Then the family moved on with what was left of the Martin/Willey Handcart Company. Upon arrival in the Salt Lake Valley, Langley was still alive! He was eighteen years old and weighed only sixty pounds. That eighteen-year-old boy was my great-grandfather. I'm grateful for the preservation of his young life and for the fortitude and stamina of his noble, courageous mother

who was a light to her family and kept her son going in spite of deathly odds.

You probably will not have to push a handcart in a blizzard over the Plains or save the scriptures and run away from a mob, but you may have to walk away from friends and fashions and invitations that would compromise your standards of goodness. And that takes courage. Soon you will be a member of the Relief Society and one day a mother, who must lend strength and testimony to future generations. In your preparing years you can't afford to say, "I'm going to give up. The Church standards are too high. It's too hard to live the standards of personal purity with exactness. I'm too weak." You can do it! For the sake of your future, you must do it!

Are you ready for another poem? You can probably tell that Robert Frost is one of my favorite poets.

The Road Not Taken

Two roads diverged in a yellow wood,
And sorry I could not travel both
And be one traveler, long I stood
And looked down one as far as I could
To where it bent in the undergrowth;

Then took the other, as just as fair,
And having perhaps the better claim,
Because it was grassy and wanted wear;
Though as for that the passing there
Had worn them really about the same,

And both that morning equally lay
In leaves no step had trodden black.
Oh, I kept the first for another day!
Yet knowing how way leads on to way,
I doubted if I should ever come back.

I shall be telling this with a sigh
Somewhere ages and ages hence:
Two roads diverged in a wood, and I—
I took the one less traveled by,
And that has made all the difference.[2]

Elizabeth, always remember that you too can choose the road "less traveled by," and it can make all the difference. You can live in the world but not be of the world. The Lord invites us to come out of the cold danger of worldliness and into the warmth of His light. This requires integrity, strength of character, and faith—faith in the truths taught by the Lord Jesus Christ. "I am the light of the world: he that followeth me shall not walk in darkness, but shall have the light of life" (John 8:12).

Can I suggest three things that will help you see the light and follow it in your life? First, and most important of all, pray. As you talk to your Heavenly Father and pour out your heart to Him, you will draw closer to Him. Then pause, stop, and listen to the feelings of your heart. Seek to understand the promptings of the Spirit. As you pray sincerely, you will come to feel Heavenly Father's great love for you. Second, study the scriptures. The scriptures teach us the ways of the Lord. They answer questions about how to live today. They bring a light and a spirit into our lives that we can get no other way. Third, be anxiously engaged in a good cause. That means: serve your family and friends. Be active in the Church and seminary. Develop talents and skills. Set a good example. Stand as a witness of God "at all times and in all things, and in all places." As you do that, the light will grow brighter and brighter in your life, and it will be reflected in your countenance.

The Young Women office windows look out at the holy Salt Lake Temple, and we can see brides as they come out to have pictures taken. These lovely temple-married brides all look beautiful because there is a glow in their faces and a light in their eyes. That light

comes from their understanding of the influence of the Savior in their lives. There is something very special about a young woman who has prepared herself and is worthy to make sacred covenants and receive the ordinances of the temple.

Just as we followed the light of a truck one stormy winter night, so did Caroline and Mary Elizabeth and Jane follow the light of the Lord, and so can you. And when you come to those times that will require courage and strength and faith, remember the words of the hymn:

> The Lord is my light; then why should I fear?
> By day and by night his presence is near.[3]

Have you had experiences that required courage and personal strength? It would be so inspiring to hear from you about that. Would you please share it with me?

Dear Elizabeth, my friend, the Lord is always there to help you. The example of His life and His teachings are a steady, sure guide. We can follow Him with confidence and perfect trust, for He is our Savior. I love Him.

And I love you,

Your friend

chapter twelve

The Envelope

BE a goal setter

Dear Beth,

Now that's a new nickname for you, I'll bet! Has anyone ever called you that? I loved reading about your experience that required courageous action on your part. You give me so much faith in the future—because the future is you!

You are so blessed to be at the threshold of life at this very crucial time in the world's history. Imagine how Isaiah or John the Revelator would love to be alive today. This was the day they saw, the time of which they taught. We know the fulness of the gospel, we are led by a prophet, and there are abundant opportunities for young women. I hope you feel very blessed and loved by your Heavenly Father. He has sent you to earth at this crucial and exciting time because He needs your strength and your talents and your goodness.

A demanding world awaits you, and I am so proud of you for the

preparation you are making toward your own unique contribution. These are precious years. What you learn and do in the period of time between twelve and twenty-two will in large part determine the direction of the remainder of your life. You have no time to waste! No time for too much TV or too much goofing off. What you spend your time doing is what you become. You must find a way to mesh the goals you have for your life with what you are doing on a daily basis.

I have an old envelope that I treasure. I know it's old because the postage on it says "6 cents," and that means it was mailed a long time ago. On the back of this envelope are directions to a destination.

It belonged to a young couple who were then in their twenties and newly married. They were romantic and idealistic and optimistic about their future. He was in graduate school. She taught high school to support the two of them. One bright autumn day in New England, they took a picnic lunch out to Walden Pond near Boston. Because you love literature, you'll remember that Walden Pond and Henry David Thoreau go together. Like Thoreau, the couple chose this location to think and ponder on their future. The question they had come to consider was this: What should they do with their lives? They wanted a road map for the future. They had a new marriage. It was a promising partnership. The future stretched out before them, and they wanted to make the very most of it. They talked of what to do and where to live. They talked about the children they wanted to have. They wanted to develop talents and share what they had been given; they wanted to make the world better because they lived in it. They wanted to serve God always. They were goal setters. So after a very philosophical afternoon and lots of discussion, they wrote down on the back of an envelope a list of goals and hopes and dreams that they intended would set the tone for their lives together.

They drove away from that beautiful, serene setting with hope and optimism . . . and the envelope. The practical, routine, daily things of life took over. The envelope was soon forgotten. They got caught up in life. They prayed often and worked hard and served

others. They started their family and finished graduate school. He worked at his career. She worked at being a young mother. They served—both in their Church and in the community. They had more children. Life got busier and busier. They didn't think about their Walden Pond envelope much at all. Things weren't so philosophical, but they were happy. They were very happy. They just kept trying, with each choice they made, to see which path God wanted them to take.

Many years passed. They faced trials; some of them were very hard ones. There were a variety of challenges. Some could have broken their spirits. Now they were middle-aged and they kept plucking gray hairs and watching their waistlines expand. They moved to a new city where the husband was hired at a responsible job.

One day in the process of the move, the wife found, among some long-forgotten papers, the Walden Pond envelope. It was old and yellowed. On the back was the list of "goals" made by the young newlywed couple so many, many years before.

As she read down the list, tears came to her eyes. The years flashed by since they had spent that long-ago afternoon at Walden Pond. As her eyes focused on each item, she realized that most of the goals on the list had come to pass. Interestingly enough, her husband's new job was the fulfillment of the final notation they had made at Walden Pond. It was time to get a new envelope and make a new list.

I assume that you might have your own envelope, so to speak. If, for some reason, you haven't gone through the process of thoughtfully preparing written goals, I counsel you to do it now. You will go places and do things and have experiences that I cannot even imagine. But you must be working at something worthy of your best effort. You can't just expect the Lord to come along and pluck you off the couch and set you on a path of achievement. He doesn't work that way. He can direct effort, but he can't direct inertia!

Let me tell you about my friend Dan, who was once a ski instructor and had an interesting experience with a goal setter. He said that

at the beginning of each day of instruction all the ski instructors met together to determine who would teach each class. No one wanted the beginners. Everyone looked forward to teaching the intermediate and advanced students. It just so happened that on this day, my friend Dan drew the assignment to teach the beginners. Disappointed, but being a good sport, he went out to meet his class.

It was a mixed group of all ages and it was a typical day on the slopes. There was one participant that stood out in the group. He was a very determined seventy-five-year-old man. At the end of the day, my friend Dan rode the ski lift with this fine gentleman and was intrigued by the conversation they had. "Here is someone very special," he thought to himself, "Who is he?" As the group departed that day, Dan observed this man take out of his wallet a tattered piece of paper and scratch through an item of what appeared to be a list.

Dan dared to ask him what this list was. The seventy-five-year-old man explained that long ago, as a young person, he had made a list of goals he wanted to accomplish in his life. Learning to ski was on his list. Then, as he put the tattered list back into his wallet, he thanked Dan for his lesson. They shook hands and, as he left, he handed Dan his card, saying, "If I can ever be of help to you give me a call." As he walked away, Dan looked at the card and, to his amazement, on the card was the name of Lowell Thomas.

This man was a world-class explorer, a geographer, and a famous news commentator. And today, at age seventy-five, he had accomplished the last on a long list of goals he had made as a youth! It was time to get a new piece of paper and start a new list.

As you set goals and work hard, remember this: There really is a law of the harvest. It's unrealistic to suppose that lofty goals and ambitions can be met without hard work, discipline, and focused effort. So, each day, each step along the way, ask for, then listen for divine guidance. Work hard at the goals you've set for yourself, then the Lord will bless you in your efforts. He will guide you to the place He needs you to be to do the things He has for you to do. The combination of directed effort on your part and living close to the Spirit will get you to where you really should be.

Right now you are at such a wonderful place in life—you have mainly yourself to work on. This is your time of personal development. This moment in your life will never happen again. Make the most of it so there will be no regrets. "Of all sad words of tongue and pen the saddest are these, it might have been."

I think I know the secret to a life of accomplishment. You need to have a vision of what you would like to become, work to make your dream a reality, and be a goal setter. Have you ever thought about your goals for the future? What kind of a person would you like to be? Do you have an ideal to follow? I would love to have you share your thinking on this in your next letter.

With great expectations and love,

Your friend

chapter thirteen

Love Learning

accomplishment is attractive

Dear Liz,

Thank you for sharing your hopes and dreams with me. You have some worthy and beautiful goals. I'm so proud of you! You can start now to make your dreams become a reality in your life. In this way you will begin preparing that wonderful gift to bring back home to Heavenly Father.

One of the finest contributions you can make to the brightness of the coming years is to get a fine education. Be qualified to do something useful. Develop a useful skill. There may be time before you have a family that you will have an opportunity to work in a career. More than likely, there will be many years after your family is raised, should that blessing come to you, that you can resume opportunities in the world of work. The time could come in your life when you will need to provide for yourself or your family. That could happen for

numerous reasons. Life is unpredictable and, as I've written to you before, I have always felt that my education was the best insurance policy I could invest in.

Beyond that, what a blessing it is for a child to have a mother who knows something! Fortunate is a husband who has a wife who is educated. Someone he can talk to about ideas. This is especially important if your husband is educated, because he will appreciate a partner he has something in common with intellectually.

Regarding the importance of education, President Gordon B. Hinckley has said: "You need to increase your education, to refine your skills, to hone your abilities so that you may fill responsibilities of consequence in the society of which you will become a part."[1]

I sat with some seventeen-year-old girls recently just to visit. I like to try and understand young women and their concerns. I asked them where they saw themselves in two years. One said, "Not in school! I can hardly wait to get out of high school!"

"Then what will you do?" I asked, curious to know.

"I'll get married or something," was her reply. I was concerned that this young woman didn't have a clear vision of her future and all the preparation it will take on her part to make it a masterpiece. I asked her, "What kind of boy will you marry next year or the next? What will you do after you two are married? What do you want your children to be like?" Those are all-important questions for you to consider. Your choices today affect your future and that, my friend, will probably include more than you.

I agree, not everyone is a great student. But you can do well at something. You have talents waiting for discovery and development. Do you know what they are? How can they help you in your future role? You were sent here to succeed. You were sent here to learn the joy of doing your best. With the help of family, friends, teachers, and your best friend of all, your Heavenly Father, you will succeed.

My dear friend, Elizabeth, for you this is a time of unprecedented opportunities and options. You have important choices to make.

Please, for yourself and your future family, choose the finest education you can obtain, for "when you educate a man you educate an individual, but when you educate a woman you educate a whole family."[2] I think I can see in you, even now, a young woman who is trying to get a good education and is preparing to bless her future family.

The joy of living in a happy, productive home environment in the years to come is dependent on the creators of that home. Let me tell you about Alice.

Alice is happily married and the mother of six children. She is also trained as a pediatrician. She has served in many ways in the Church, including in the Relief Society presidency, and is currently a Cub Scout leader. She sews Halloween costumes and volunteers in the science lab at the elementary school.

Right now Alice is a full-time mother. Undoubtedly, she will return to her medical practice when her children are raised, but that doesn't mean that she isn't using her medical education now. Teenagers from the neighborhood have been known to appear on her porch with all kinds of symptoms, including acute appendicitis and a strangulated hernia. One dramatic event occurred when a vacationing Mom telephoned Alice. Her daughter's baby-sitter had reported that the little girl was coughing and seemed sick. After apologizing for bothering her, the Mom asked Alice for a favor. Could she find time during the afternoon to check on her little girl who appeared to have croup? For some reason, Alice immediately put aside what she was doing and went right to the home of this little girl. She found the girl not breathing and in full cardiac arrest. She applied CPR. By the time the paramedics arrived, the child was breathing again. Alice's education and her skills saved the child's life.

How do you suppose Alice became the kind of woman she is today? What might she have done at your age to prepare for her future as a doctor, mother, wife, church worker, and school volunteer?

My guess is that she used her time wisely. She must have decided to learn well, to apply herself in school so she could pass the tests for

entrance to medical school. That meant that she gave her best efforts to studying. She took science classes, because doctors are scientists, and did well in them. In her spare time when she wasn't studying, she must have learned to sew, because she could make Halloween costumes for her children as a mom. She must have experienced the joy of service as a youth and found satisfaction in helping others. Surely this was another factor in Alice's choosing a career of service as a mother and doctor.

I have to tell you that there will be surprises and experiences in your life, both good and bad, that you can't even dream of. That's what makes life such an interesting adventure! C. S. Lewis described a wonderful idea from his friend, author George MacDonald. Listen to this:

"Imagine yourself as a living house. God comes in to rebuild that house. At first, perhaps, you can understand what He is doing. He is getting the drains right and stopping the leaks in the roof and so on: you knew that those jobs needed doing and so you are not surprised. But presently He starts knocking the house about in a way that hurts abominably and does not seem to make sense. What on earth is He up to? The explanation is that He is building quite a different house from the one you thought of—throwing out a new wing here, putting on an extra floor there, running up towers, making courtyards. You thought you were going to be made into a decent little cottage: but He is building a palace. He intends to come and live in it Himself."[3]

We don't want to willfully set goals for ourselves with no thought of what God might have for us to do. Pray for divine guidance so that Heavenly Father can direct your efforts in a path that will bless you.

And don't forget your earthly parents, who also can guide and direct you as you get an education and learn new things. I remember well my first few weeks of living away from home and at college. They were hard. I struggled a bit and I was naive. I had come from a small town that didn't even have one stoplight. Fortunately I didn't have a car, so I didn't have to worry about stoplights. At least that's one

worry I didn't have! My mother had made our home an easy, wonderful place to live. She had fixed delicious meals. She had inspired me. My Dad had provided financial security and wise counsel. But suddenly I was on my own, and there were decisions to make, papers to write, exams to take, classes to prepare for, laundry to do, meals to fix, Church assignments to fulfill, and an expanding social life to keep track of. There were new roommates. It was difficult—some days nothing went well. After one such day, I called my mother and said, "This is just too hard! If you think college is so great, why don't you come and take my place? I bet I could get my old job back at the Dairy Queen on Main Street." She listened quietly. Mother was very wise but not very sympathetic. She simply said, "Well, dear, you'd better learn to handle it, because it gets harder!"

She was so right. Gradually I did learn to organize myself and I learned a lot of other things, too. I changed my mind about wanting to give up college and go back to where everything was familiar and easy. I'm so thankful I stayed and did something that was hard for me. From those demanding experiences I began to mature.

Elder Glenn L. Pace tells a wonderful story that illustrates my point. He says:

"When I was in junior high school, I would get out of bed on cold winter mornings and head for the heat vent to get warm. The family cat would always beat me there, so I would gently shoo her away and sit down. Soon my mother would tell me it was time to leave for school. I would look out at the icicles on the house and dread going out into the cold, let alone beginning another day of school.

"As I kissed my mother good-bye and went out the door, I would look longingly at my comfortable spot in front of the heat vent and find that the cat had repossessed it. How I envied that cat! If that weren't enough, she would look up at me with heavy eyelids and an expression that seemed to laugh at me and say, 'Have fun at school, Glenn. I'm sure glad I'm not a human.' I hated it when she did that.

"However, an interesting thing would happen as the day went on.

I would come home after experiencing the joys and sorrows of the school day and see that lazy cat still curled up in front of the vent, and I would smile and say to her, 'I'm sure glad I'm not a cat.'"[4]

Leaving that heat vent took discipline on cold mornings. Maturing and growing requires discipline and can be uncomfortable. But how unfortunate it would be to waste these growing moments. As you concentrate on developing a wide variety of skills, your life will be forever blessed. We all need to use our time wisely. Now is the time to get an education and to develop some skills that will make an eternal difference.

What are some of the practical skills you are trying to develop in your life? Who is helping you? Are you having fun as you work on them? What are your educational goals? Do you want to go to college or trade school? I hope you'll share in your next letter.

Hoping that you will have a love affair with learning, I remain,

Your friend

chapter fourteen

Socially Skillful

"DO ye even so to them"

Dear Elizabeth,

In my last letter I talked about getting an education. But there are other things to learn that are also very important—social skills. You'd be amazed at the difference it makes to develop good social skills. Your own trip through life can be much smoother; and good social skills can help you make things smoother for everyone else too.

It's unfortunate that the trend in the world today is to demand rights, accuse others, and excuse ourselves. The Savior taught us to care for others, to bless their lives, to understand their needs, to be humble and meek, merciful and kind. Remember when Jesus was mourning the death of His beloved cousin John the Baptist. He was sorrowing; He was sad; and He wanted to go away and be alone. "He departed thence by ship into a desert place apart: and when the people had heard thereof, they followed him on foot out of the cities.

And Jesus went forth, and saw a great multitude, and was moved with compassion toward them, and he healed their sick. . . . His disciples came to him, saying, . . . [S]end the multitude away, that they may . . . buy themselves victuals. But Jesus said unto them, They need not depart; give ye them to eat" (Matthew 14:13–16). Jesus forgot about His own concerns and fed the five thousand with five loaves of bread and two fishes. He was the perfect exemplar of caring for others. He taught, "Blessed are the poor in spirit who come unto me, for theirs is the kingdom of heaven. . . . And blessed are the meek, for they shall inherit the earth. . . . And blessed are the merciful, for they shall obtain mercy. And blessed are all the pure in heart, for they shall see God. And blessed are all the peacemakers, for they shall be called the children of God" (3 Nephi 12: 3, 5, 7–9). He taught us to be peacemakers. You can't beat those items for social skills! And He promises us rewards for those behaviors. We will have mercy. We will inherit the earth. We will see God. What a remarkable reward!

It has been my privilege to know people who possess these qualities. Let me tell you about two. The first was tall and a bit round. She was older. Her smile exuded warmth. She had such a pleasant sense of humor. She was capable. She was kind. I don't know that she was born with those qualities, but I do know that they were well developed because she practiced them constantly. She nurtured her sense of humor by laughing at things that were funny and making light of things that didn't really matter. I can still remember her chuckle and lighthearted laugh. When she didn't marry or have children, she didn't mope away her life. She was productive in her career and in the community. She was elected to the city council. She held positions of respect in organizations she belonged to. At Christmastime, she got a list of all the children in her small town and sent Santa Claus letters. She didn't have her own children, so she found little girls who were needy and bought dolls for them; she gave remote-controlled cars to the little boys. She was happy, and others were happy because of her.

The second is a young friend of our family. Kids love to be around this teenager because she thinks their witty remarks are *so* funny! She makes them feel confident, and they like to spend time with her because of that. She doesn't think they are dumb or stupid (secret fears many of us have). She is warm and accepting. This is a social skill. It is a Christlike quality.

Oh, Elizabeth, how skills such as these—social skills—will bless you in your life, in public service, in a career, as a parent, as a spouse, as a Church worker. Think of talking to a boss, or going to a parent-teacher conference, or speaking with the zoning commission, or with the ward correlation council, having a desire to be warm, to understand, to be helpful rather than self-centered and combative and defensive and always so very right! Can you see how developing good social skills can bless lives, including your own?

You may recall a story told about President Kimball when he helped a woman in an airport. She was tending a two-year-old and was pregnant with another. This act of kindness is often told, but let me share with you the result of that kindness in a letter President Kimball received more than twenty years later:

"Dear President Kimball:

"I am a student at Brigham Young University. I have just returned from my mission in Munich, West Germany. I had a lovely mission and learned much. . . .

"I was sitting in priesthood meeting last week, when a story was told of a loving service which you performed some twenty-one years ago in the Chicago airport. The story told of how you met a young pregnant mother with a . . . screaming child, in . . . distress, waiting in a long line for her tickets. She was threatening miscarriage and therefore couldn't lift her child to comfort her. She had experienced four previous miscarriages, which gave added reason for the doctor's orders not to bend or lift.

"You comforted the crying child and explained the dilemma to

the other passengers in line. This act of love took the strain and tension off my mother. I was born a few months later in Flint, Michigan.

"I just want to *thank you* for your love. *Thank you* for your example!"[1]

Good social skills come from the simple statement in Matthew 7:12, which we call the Golden Rule: "Whatsoever ye would that men should do to you, do ye even so to them."

How do you treat others? Could you share your thoughts on this in your next letter? Do you think of others first? Are you warm and interested in other people? Do you know someone who knows how to listen, really listen, with her heart? Does she go beyond just being kind and pleasant and, in addition, listen to real needs and try to help? Does she focus attention on the other person rather than on herself? Doing so can give you a feeling of freedom and allow you to forget yourself and your own needs and inadequacies and care for another person. People who can do that are loved, and they are happy. There is opportunity everywhere to brush up on our social skills! I'm still practicing. Practice makes perfect, they say!

With joy in polishing up that golden rule, and with love,

Your friend

chapter fifteen

We Seek After These Things

"... virtuous, lovely, or of good report or praiseworthy"

Dear Beth,

I love the name Beth; it is so pretty. That is what we call my cousin whose name is Elizabeth. What nicknames do you use? Which ones do you like best?

I remember when I began dating Steve, who would become my husband. I was thrilled to know that he was student body vice president of culture at the university we attended! Wow! I romantically envisioned a constant round of evenings at the theater, concerts, art exhibits, and ballets with this exciting man. Perhaps I had a somewhat naive and idealistic view of life. Still, I know there is something in us that is better and finer when we are exposed to the arts and cultural events. I'm grateful that my husband enjoys these things with me and encourages them in our home. I must confess that the title "cultural vice president" may well have been "false advertising." After

we really got acquainted, I learned that he prefers athletic events to concerts. Yet he attends and enjoys concerts, and that well rounded-ness is attractive to me.

It is a joy to me when one of our sons takes a date to a symphony performance after playing a muddy, mean rugby game. We introduced our seven sons to the symphony by taking them to an outdoor performance of the *1812 Overture*, complete with live cannon fire at the end.

This caught their attention!

Perhaps like your parents, we've spent thousands of dollars on music lessons and spent untold hours practicing piano and violin at our house. A favorite memory of mine is of one of our little boys sitting on the piano bench with his ball mitt next to him and his cleated feet swinging in time to the music he played. One time one of our sons said, "Boy, if I only had one hour left to live, I'd spend it practicing the piano, because those practice hours last forever." Beautiful music can enrich your home and the lives of those who can play and create it.

What about art? Even if you can't paint artistically, you can learn to appreciate it. If you don't play or sing musically, you can develop a taste for the beauty of it. My favorite free-time pursuit is great literature. I love to curl up with a good book and have been known to do so late at night and early into the morning. President Gordon B. Hinckley said: "I have in my home a reasonably good sound system. I do not use it frequently, but now and again, I sit quietly in the semi-darkness and listen for an hour or so to music that has endured through the centuries because of its remarkable qualities. I listened the other evening to Beethoven's Concerto for the Violin and marveled that such a thing could come out of the mind of a man. The composer, I suppose, was very much like the rest of us. I do not know how tall he was or how broad he was or how much he weighed. I assume that he got hungry, felt pain, and had most of the problems that we all have, and maybe some that we do not have. But out of the

genius of that mind came a tremendous blending to create rare and magnificent masterpieces of music."[1]

A Young Women leader once told me that when she was a Laurel her stake had been given an opportunity to join with other stakes to sing with a large chorus in a Church music festival. Each ward had been assigned to learn certain songs; they had had rehearsals as a stake, and then had met with other stakes to sing in a wonderful music festival. She still remembers that while she was singing in that grand chorus, the Spirit bore powerful testimony to her that what they were singing was truth. Ever since then, it has been a reference point in her testimony. She says that it was one of the definitive memories of her Young Women experience. A musical experience. The Spirit bore witness to her through music.

I remember a wedding luncheon that we enjoyed recently. The food had been delicious, and was beautifully served. It was a quiet opportunity to bask in the beauty of a temple marriage ceremony held earlier that morning. There was an intimate group of family and close friends in attendance. Then, the adoring, handsome groom requested that his bride play the piano for us, and she agreed to do so.

She played with such grace and elegance that we all melted as we listened to her. We loved the music she made. As she played I couldn't help but look at her mother—she was weeping. It touched my heart to observe this tender moment. Later, this mother recounted how she had awakened every morning to Melissa's music on the piano, and today it had suddenly struck her that those mornings were now for Tom and Melissa's new family. She will not live in her parents' house now. Her music will fill her own home, and her own husband and family will awaken to her piano music. Sad? Yes. Wonderful? Yes. The plan? For sure!

Refinement can add a gentle spirit to a home. What are your views on this subject? Have you been trying to cultivate a spirit of refinement in your life? It is a gift worth cultivating, Elizabeth. Write to me about the songs you love. Do you like to read? Write about your favorite books. Perhaps you have a favorite poem? Wouldn't it be lovely to memorize a short poem, perhaps something by Robert Frost or Elizabeth Barrett Browning? Such an undertaking could add a nice touch of class to your personality.

Here's to refinement and all things beautiful. With love,

Your friend

chapter sixteen

To Everyone a Gift Is Given

"That all may be profited"

Dear Elizabeth,

Can I tell you a story about my own girlhood?

It was a warm, lazy summer afternoon—the usual. Not much was happening when some friends appeared at my door. We had soon cooked up some fun plans for the afternoon. I ran to tell Mom of my plan and whereabouts. It was fine with her if I went, she said, but she did want to remind me of the essay contest I'd been interested in. Isn't that just the way with moms? They are in tune with things of importance, which can put a damper on the most exciting plans!

I then remembered that the deadline was tomorrow. It looked like I'd have to make a choice between my friends and a boring old essay that I hadn't even written yet. I could play, or I could sit at the table all afternoon with my pen in hand. It was not a hard choice for me!

But for Mother, it wasn't that simple. She often served as my conscience and helped me see things more clearly.

Mother was good at sorting out things—all kinds of things—like feelings and priorities. So we had one of those sorting-things-out conversations. I slowly moped back to my friends and explained how much I'd love to go with them but that, sadly, I had forgotten a commitment I'd made.

I didn't tell them it was a commitment to myself that I was going to honor. They would have thought I was a real nerd. Instead, I did tell them if they ran into any cute boys to be sure to say, "Hi" from me. I was sure they would!

In some ways it was not fun to sit there alone that afternoon and stare at a blank page I needed to fill. But to tell the truth, once I began, I forgot my sacrifice, and ideas began to flow. Some of them were even kind of fun to see in writing.

After much effort, several rewrites, and much refining, the essay was completed. I had addressed the contest theme, had managed to come up with the right number of words, and had met the deadline for submission! I stuck my entry in the mail and soon forgot about it as other activities crowded into my life and took up my attention.

Several weeks passed. And then one day in the mail I received notice that I'd won the district essay contest. The letter said, "Congratulations, we've sent your essay to the state finals!"

"Well, that's nice," I thought. "I guess it was worth it!" and I ran to answer the phone. My friends had something else in mind—swimming I think. At least I hadn't lost any friends over the essay afternoon.

Not long after that, the most amazing thing happened. I was notified that I was the state winner of the essay contest. The prize included various things, among them was a savings bond worth money! (I could cash it in immediately and have the money instantly or let it mature and have a larger amount.)

I thought about that decision a while. To write the essay, I had

been willing to put off some instant pleasure (like spending that fun afternoon with my friends) to have a greater reward later. I learned from that experience that it's good to have goals, to set a few priorities, and then make a little sacrifice to accomplish them.

That's not to say for one second that friends aren't worthwhile. They are. Friends are the best; but life constantly offers choices. Sometimes we have to choose between two good things. Sometimes one of those is easy and the other one requires some effort. At times like that it takes self-discipline, effort, a conscience, and/or a good mom!

Life is like that. There will always be choices to make, and your choices will make all the difference.

I had no idea that the experience of writing an essay would turn into such an important skill or talent. I found that I enjoy writing short stories, essays, and poetry. Eventually I became editor of the school newspaper, and later I loved teaching high school English. Today, in my calling as Young Women general president, I write all the time! I write letters to the leaders of young women, young women themselves, and to other Church leaders. Then there are the talks I get to write . . . oh, so many of them.

The day I chose to spend some time with a pencil and paper instead of my friends has had far-reaching consequences that I couldn't foresee when I was fifteen!

In fact, one day soon after I received the call to serve as general president, I was feeling surprised and even overwhelmed. I remarked to my mother, who, by the way, is very wise, "I wish I'd had any idea or hint or indication that I would be called upon to do something like this."

Her remark to me was this, "Dear, if you had known, how would you have prepared differently?"

I have thought about that so many times since that day.

Could I ask you this question, If you knew what life had in store for you, just how would you prepare? Think about that. No one knows what lies ahead, but we do know that there are so many opportunities

that lie within our grasp. It would turn out to be a great blessing if we determined here and now that we would take advantage of every opportunity we could. A fine motto for a teenage girl could be, "Prepare today!"

Elizabeth, please write back regarding your thoughts on preparation for the future by developing all the talents you can. I'll be patiently awaiting your response as I remain,

Your friend

chapter seventeen

Did You Think to Pray?

Then did you stop to listen?

Dear Liz,

We have shared ideas with each other about some of the gifts and talents one should focus on to be well prepared and to make the most of this life. I am grateful, Elizabeth, for your willingness to be honest with me and share some heartfelt feelings. Thank you!

Of all the qualities you can develop that will bless your life and give you strength when you need it, the most important quality is spirituality. It is a natural gift from heaven that young women like you seem to have in extra measure. Girls are somehow in tune with things of the Spirit. It is a blessing to cultivate.

A pattern or blueprint for developing qualities that will invite spirituality is outlined in the 88th section of the Doctrine and Covenants. Verse 119 reads: "Organize yourselves; prepare every needful thing; and establish a house, even a house of prayer, a house

of fasting, a house of faith, a house of learning, a house of glory, a house of order, a house of God."

This verse refers specifically to a temple, but it can also refer to the home in which your family—and the Spirit—dwells. Right now you don't really have a house of your very own to work on, but you do have your own wonderful life and a special place where you sleep and keep your things. You could follow the Lord's advice and establish a room, or a nook, where you pray and ponder, where you study the scriptures and exercise your faith in the Lord.

I know a young woman who lived like this in her room. She is fourteen. Read what she wrote to the *New Era* magazine about what happened in the sacred space she had organized and prepared for herself.

Here is Katie's story:

"A while ago, I was struggling with some decisions about whether to follow the ways of the world, or to follow my beliefs. The more popular decisions weren't necessarily the ones my parents would have wanted me to choose. At the same time, I wanted to be accepted by my friends. Finally, I decided to pray for help to make the right decision. After pouring my heart out to the Lord, I received an answer saying, 'read.'

"I decided I must have been imagining the answer because reading had nothing to do with my problem. I ignored the prompting and got into bed. After several minutes, I again felt, 'read.' I received this impression several times and ignored it until I finally decided to read for a few minutes. I pulled a book off the shelf and looked at a page.

"My mind wandered, and I couldn't concentrate. Finally, I decided I had been at it long enough. I looked down to close the book and realized that the bookmark I was using had the Young Women theme on it. The phrase 'We will stand as witnesses of God at all times and in all things, and in all places' really stood out.

"It was then I realized that no matter what I decided to do, my decision would have to be something Heavenly Father would approve

of. . . . I bowed my head in prayer once again to thank Heavenly Father for the answer and to apologize for not listening the first time."[1]

Liz, do you know the hymn that begins by asking, "Ere you left your room this morning, did you think to pray?"[2]

Do you pause to listen after you pray? Have you left time in your busy, bustling schedule for quiet moments? The "whispering of the Spirit" is a still, small voice, one that isn't heard over loud, blaring music or harsh voices or frenetic activity. It is a sweet, divine gift, given to those who seek and patiently wait upon the Lord.

I remember President David O. McKay telling of the grief suffered in a family due to the loss of a precious, priceless son. His death had occurred as the result of a tragic accident, and the parents were inconsolable. The father was particularly troubled but went about his round of duties, relentlessly trying to block out his intense sorrow. One day the mother was at home quietly going about her work, and her thoughts turned toward the son they sorrowed for. And then something unusual happened. This son came to her briefly. He explained that he had tried to visit his father, whose grief was so inconsolable; but his father's life was too busy, too noisy, and he hadn't been able to get through to him. He wanted his parents to know that he was fine, that there was no need to worry about him. This spiritual experience was a great source of comfort to the mother and to the father when she recounted it to him.[3] But he learned a great lesson. Sometimes we need to be still for a moment. We need to slow down and be less frantic. The scriptures teach us, "Be still, and know that I am God" (Psalm 46:10).

Remember what Elijah learned: The Lord is not in the earthquake or in the wind. He is not in the fire. He is a still, small voice (1 Kings 19:11–12). All of us need to have more reverence in our lives, more holiness, more times of quiet and peace and calm. We need a place where our souls can be nourished and tutored and blessed. Temples are such places. Home can be such a place. Dear Elizabeth, my busy, happy, enthusiastic young friend, invite the Spirit

to abide with you and then welcome its companionship with a listening, prepared, quiet heart.

I once had an experience that I would like to share with you. I was trying to make a very important decision that concerned more than just myself. I'd had many years of practice in going to the Lord with decisions. I fasted. I attended temple sessions. I prayed a great deal. I tried to be spiritually in tune. Then I made the decision and took it to the Lord for confirmation. In spite of all my spiritual preparations, I still felt unsettled with the final decision. Then I read in the Doctrine and Covenants 9:7: "Behold, you have not understood; you have supposed that I would give it unto you, when you took no thought save it was to ask me."

It became very clear to me that to be completely settled about my decision, I needed more than spiritual preparation. I needed to do some practical preparation. I got up from my knees and got to work. I met with people. I gathered data. I analyzed it. I thought about it. I counseled with Church leaders. I counseled with family. I considered it thoughtfully and very prayerfully. I wrote things down. Using a paper and pencil is always useful to me in analyzing information. It clarifies my thinking. So I wrote lists of pros and cons and considered these prayerfully, crossing things off, narrowing things down. I didn't hurry. I took time to let things settle in my mind. Then, in due time, I knew what I should do. Finally, the Lord blessed me with peace about the matter, just as promised in D&C 6:23: "Did I not speak peace to your mind concerning the matter? What greater witness can you have than from God?" I learned that inspiration comes during this process. Can these same steps apply to you in major decisions you make? Surely they can.

Let me share another example. A young couple had a decision to make concerning a financial matter. Together they researched all the options. They investigated the matter inside out. The husband was well educated in financial and business matters and put his best thinking and analyzing to work. The final decision had to be made at open

of business on Tuesday. On Monday night as the couple knelt together in prayer, they presented their decision to the Lord. They explained that they had used all their own data-gathering, analysis, and logic resources. They had done all they could think of and this seemed to be the course to take. But they recognized that Heavenly Father knows all things, and so they pleaded that if there were some piece of information that would impact the decision, would the Lord please bring it to their attention. They retired for the night feeling fine about their decision and also about what they had asked of the Lord. Early the next morning, they were awakened by the phone ringing. The person on the other end gave them information regarding their decision that they had had no way of knowing. But this information clearly changed the decision that they would make. By opening of business that day, they knew what to do. It proved to be correct as the years passed and time confirmed their choice. The Lord did help them after they had done all they could do themselves.

Let's look at the steps taken in these two examples: First, the person gathered information thoughtfully and thoroughly. Second, the person prayerfully analyzed the information gathered. Third, the person sought counsel from leaders and from family, which he thoughtfully and humbly considered. (It is important to be humble and teachable. A willful person has a hard time taking counsel. But remember this one word of caution: It is important to learn to be spiritually self-reliant. We certainly don't need to run to our bishops with everything. While, in major matters, it is wise to counsel with one you trust, bishops don't and can't make decisions for you. Decisions are for you to make after all is said and done.) Fourth, the person made a decision, then humbly and prayerfully took the decision to the Lord. And fifth, the Lord answered with peace to the soul.

This is not to say that if we pray hard and do what is right, we are never going to have a bad outcome. We're on this earth to have experience. Those experiences aren't always the ones we would choose for ourselves, but we're more likely to fulfill His purposes and our own

goals if we develop the faith to know that after all we can do, God will bless our experiences to our good. The Lord will help you after you have done all you can do in making decisions and in all you do to serve Him and His children.

Do you love the Savior, the Lord Jesus Christ? Do you understand what He did for you and what He will do for you?

Read the Gospel of John from start to finish. Then read the other Gospels—Matthew, Mark, Luke. Then read Third Nephi, starting in chapter eleven. Learn of Christ. Thank God for His life and for His perfect love for you and for His perfect example. Then try to follow it. Try to live like He taught. Try to ask, "What would the Savior do?" and then do it. Try to always remember what He did for you. Remember His atoning sacrifice and never mock it by your actions, but glorify His name by your actions. When we partake of the sacrament each week, we should all be reminded of how He has blessed us. If we thoughtfully listen to the words of those prayers and live worthily to take His name upon us, we will be blessed and we will bless others. If we love the Lord, we will reverence Him and worship Him, and our reverence will be observed in our actions and attitudes.

There is a story told of a family who was investigating the Church. This couple came to church one Sunday at the invitation of the missionaries. With great expectations, the missionaries stood by the door to welcome them. There was the usual friendly and sociable spirit in the rented hall where this small branch held their meetings. The members talked noisily one with another. When this family came into the room, they quietly moved toward some chairs, knelt for a moment, and closed their eyes in a word of prayer. Then they sat in an attitude of reverence in the midst of all the commotion. They had come to what they regarded as a worship service, and they behaved themselves accordingly.

At the close of the meeting, they left quietly, and when they next met with the missionaries, they spoke of their disappointment in what they had experienced.

Reverence. Remember, reverence.

Elizabeth, tonight when you kneel in your private prayer, remember to give thanks for all you have been given because you are so very blessed. Heavenly Father will continue to give to you. Let Him help you be all that you can be and help you do all that you can do.

I bear testimony of our Heavenly Father's great goodness and love and pray for Him to help you meet your bright future well equipped and with confidence.

I would love it if you felt safe enough to share your testimony of spiritual matters in a letter to me, Elizabeth. Acknowledging our gratitude and love for the Lord and His blessings to us is pleasing to Him. Always remember the importance of having an attitude of gratitude for all that we are blessed with. I remain gratefully,

Your friend

chapter eighteen

Taste the Sweetness of Service

"AS ye have done it unto one of the least of these, . . . ye have done it unto me."

Dear Liz,

I get the impression that you enjoy giving of yourself to others. What a wonderful quality that is to develop! It is truly a talent, I believe. I know someone who prays each morning that Heavenly Father will help her know who she can help that day. Wow! That is impressive!

As you are considering Personal Progress value experiences, value projects, or other service opportunities, consider visiting with the Relief Society president. Ask, "Is there something that a young woman like me can do to help with the compassionate service in our ward?" I can just hear a grateful Relief Society president say, "Oh, what a blessing it would be if some girls would go visit Sister Wood who has had a stroke. Sister Wood taught high school English for twenty-five years. She loves youth. She loves literature. She loves learning. The stroke has left Sister Wood blind and completely bedridden and helpless. What a blessing it would be if girls would go to her home. Two girls could go together following the pattern of visiting teaching. Go together and read to Sister Wood on a regular basis. She would look forward to that. It would brighten her day. It would lift her spirits. It would bless her life." Just imagine what it would do for you, the giver of the service!

I can hear the Relief Society president saying to you, "Elizabeth, do you know that Sister Jones is feeling overwhelmed right now with the four preschoolers she has? It would greatly benefit that family if someone could come into that home and relieve Sister Jones for a few hours occasionally. Play with the children. Teach the children. Maybe even wash up a few dishes in the sink. Maybe even tidy up the family room." And do you know, it would bless you for doing this kind of service.

As you work to serve someone else, even your mother, or other family members, wonderful relationships can be established or enriched! Miracles can occur. You will be doing something greater than a service "project." You will be learning to serve your sisters, learning to be compassionate. You will be learning to do the work of women and looking forward to the time when you will be fully immersed in Relief Society work.

I liked the time my Laurel class prepared dinner one night for people in the neighborhood who needed a boost. The girls, giggles and all, met at our home. Everybody brought pre-assigned ingredients for the recipes. Together we all worked and laughed and talked. As we cooked, Sara told us about the man who had run into her car yesterday. Amy laughed about a prank that had been played on her. We all contributed stories as we made a delicious salad, cooked vegetables, and prepared a chicken dish. Dessert was apple crisp. The girls even peeled the apples—fresh, golden delicious apples. They made this dessert from scratch without even a can opener. These great teenagers learned about preparing a nutritious, well-balanced meal

and arranging it on the plate so it was attractive. While the food was cooking, they copied the recipes on cards and now have the beginnings of a recipe file that they can take with them into their future roles as homemakers.

When the food preparation was complete, the girls piled into cars and delivered their gift of love. At one home they visited an older gentleman who spent the days with his wife in a rest home, then came home in the evening with a heavy heart to a dark, empty house. When the young women rang his doorbell and delivered their warm dinner to him, he was delighted! He was overjoyed, in fact! He praised them for what they had done and was so grateful. With tears in his eyes, he thanked them for thinking of him.

It was really special whenever this good high priest saw the young women at church; he always had something kind to say to them, and the girls took an interest in his life. The time came when his dear wife passed away, and their hearts were touched because their friend had lost his sweetheart of fifty-four years. There were a lot of good things that came from this activity. The girls truly tasted the sweetness of service.

Tell me about service opportunities you have had. How did they make you feel? Have you wondered why you felt as you did? I can't wait for your response! Write back soon.

With love,

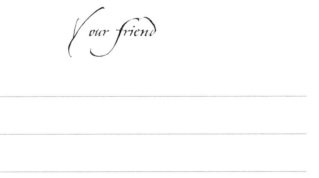

Your friend

chapter nineteen

Role Models

"each life that touches ours for good"

Dear Liz,

Just as I suspected, you have truly tasted of the sweetness of service! Thanks for giving me a "flavor" of what you did.

I was recently in a meeting where a young Laurel stood to speak. She paid tribute to her adviser as she expressed how much she loved her. She said, "I want to grow up to be just like Sister Lalli." This particular young woman doesn't have a mother to pattern her life after. She is living with people who are antagonistic toward the Church. She is the only member of the Church in that household. It means so much to her to have a righteous, loving example in her life.

During the course of her remarks, she thanked the Young Women president, who calls to check on her often, just to make sure everything is going fine. It is a great tribute to you when someone wants to be like you.

Do you have a role model, Liz? Someone who has qualities you would like to have in your own life? Maybe your ideal is your mother. Maybe there is more than one woman or girl you admire.

There are worthy women who are good examples all around us. I have been inspired throughout my life by noble women and I have tried to emulate their admirable qualities. I am grateful to them—and they do not even know about it!

My best role model has been my very own dear mother. I have tried always to be more like her because she is lovely, she is beautiful, she is kind and loving. She has worn out her life in the service of her family and many others who call her blessed. She is the hardest worker! She can still work circles around everyone I know! Mother is loyal to her family, to my father, to our Church, and to the community where she has spent her entire life. She is creative and talented. When the stake presidency called her to produce a stake pageant for Pioneer Day, she proceeded to give it everything she had. That small "stake pageant" grew to large proportions in just a few short years and is today the well-known Mormon Miracle Pageant, which has been staged for the past thirty-three years on Temple Hill in Manti, Utah. Every summer it plays to huge audiences proclaiming the message of the restored gospel of Jesus Christ. Each summer the total audiences include one hundred thousand people for eight days of its run. It has kindled and strengthened countless testimonies of performers and audiences alike.

When Mother was honored as the Mother of the Year for the state of Utah, we all knew that she was an ideal role model others could follow. By emulating the example of this lovely, faithful, noble woman, many lives have been blessed.

There is a classic story by Nathaniel Hawthorne about a young boy whose life was inspired by a great stone face. Ernest grew up looking at a mountain above his village on which appeared the likeness of a great man. Village tradition held that one day someone would come into the village who looked just like the "Great Stone Face"

and would reflect the character traits ascribed to this ideal image. Over the years, three men came to the village, and some villagers thought that in these men they would see the living likeness of the "Great Stone Face." But each time, the true character of the men disappointed the people. In the meantime, good, honest, Ernest, who lived humbly amongst the townspeople, grew in wisdom and in stature, and his appearance began to take on that of the image he had loved, looked for, and pondered on every day. And then one day, it was clear to everyone that Ernest—wise, revered Ernest—had a face like unto the "Great Stone Face" on the mountain. In the end, Ernest developed character that was true to the goodness he wanted to emulate.[1]

Sometimes we can find qualities in those closer to our own age that inspire us and make us better people. Mary Ann is a teenage girl who inspires others. She was a senior student in a math class with Emily, who was a sweet sophomore girl from a less active family. The seating arrangement in class was such that Emily sat not far from Mary Ann. There were a couple of guys that would curse and use inappropriate language during class. Some of the kids would just sit and laugh at these guys, while others tried to ignore them. One day, Mary Ann, in her own special way, told these young guys that their language was offensive and that the people around them would appreciate it if they would stop. Emily could hardly believe it! She said she almost stopped breathing. She looked at Mary Ann and there was just something about her that "glowed." Emily said, "She looked so beautiful." And the guys in the class? It was like their tongues were bound.

Emily admitted, "I don't think Mary Ann really knows me. But she makes me feel good. She really stands up for what she believes. She always makes others feel good and included." And Emily hadn't felt that for so long.

For several weeks Emily observed Mary Ann. Then one day, Mary Ann didn't show up at school. Then another, and then another. This turned into weeks. Emily overheard someone in the class say that

Mary Ann was very ill. Emily came home really upset as she had heard that her illness was life-threatening meningitis.

Emily just sat at the table crying. It wasn't like she and Mary Ann were close friends, but she said to her mom that they just had to help her! "We need to fast and pray for her!" she said. What a shock that was for the mother to hear from one of her own daughters, because fasting and prayer had not been mentioned in their home for years.

Emily and her mom talked with the rest of the family members. There was some resistance, but Emily pleaded with them. They decided that Wednesday would be the day they would fast for Mary Ann. The experience brought the most remarkable spirit of hope into the home. Because of it, some serious changes have taken place in that home. They are now having family prayer, something that had not happened for years.

After some time, Emily came home from school so excited to tell her mother that Mary Ann was back at school. A couple of days later, Emily asked her mom to come pick her up after school so she could point out Mary Ann. Her mom agreed to. As she was waiting for Emily in front of the school she saw a group of girls coming out, and she thought to herself that Mary Ann had to be in that group. Emily jumped in the car and said, "Mom, there she is!" Her mother knew which young woman she was before Emily even told her. She stood tall and beautiful, not only on the outside. She "glowed," just like Emily said.

You know the scripture that talks about "receiving his image in your countenance?" (Alma 5:14, 19). I think this is what Emily is referring to when she describes Mary Ann's "glow." And it is catching! Out of small things, great things happen.

If she were reading this, I would like to say, "Mary Ann, please let me thank you for being a wonderful role model. By your actions you have blessed at least one whole family whom you probably do not even know. And who knows how many others have been guided by your 'glow' of goodness."

Most people don't ever know that they are role models for some-one else, I suppose. But have there been role models in your life who have helped you be better and do better? Think about it. I'd be most grateful if you would be willing to share an insight or two with me regarding the role models in your life.

Please know that I'll be trying to be better, my friend, just in case someone is watching, someone who needs a little "glow" to shine their way. I remain,

Your friend

chapter twenty

Preparing to Make Sacred Covenants

A sweet, holy day for a young woman prepared

Dear Elizabeth,

Because you asked, I would love to tell you how I feel about the temple. My feelings about the temple began with the building itself. There are landmarks associated with the town where we live, and when we are getting close to home we see the landmark and know that home isn't far away. What do you look for as you return home from a trip?

The landmark in my small hometown is the beautiful Manti Temple, built on a hill on the edge of the city. Whenever we would return from a trip as children, we would search the skyline for the first sighting of the temple. When we could see it, we knew we were close to home.

Ships look for a lighthouse to signal them home. Airplanes

depend on air traffic control, radar, and runway lights to guide them safely to their final destination.

In our own lives, each one of us is invited to make the temple our beacon and our goal.

The blessings of the temple will bring us to our final destination, home to Heavenly Father. In the temple, worthy members are taught about and commit to living in the ways the Lord asks us to. To be worthy to attend the temple and partake of its blessings is the highest privilege we can have on earth. It is worth living a life of cleanliness and purity, just to be worthy and feel worthy of sacred temple bless-ings. The day I actually went to the temple for my own endowment was one of the great memorable days of my life. Later, I went to the temple with my beloved sweetheart to be sealed for time and for all eternity. Because of our temple marriage, each of our seven children was born "under the covenant." We are an eternal family with loving and holy ties that will keep us together forever, according to our continuing worthiness.

The temple is a symbol of heaven here on earth. Above the doors of the temple are inscribed the words "Holiness to the Lord. The House of the Lord." The temple really is the house of the Lord. It is a place the Lord could visit because it is His holy house on earth. There is an experience recorded about one such visit of the Savior to the temple that I would like to share with you, Elizabeth.

Lorenzo Snow was still at work in his office in the Salt Lake Temple. It was dark outside, and the stars had come out. He was the fifth president of the Church, but he was also serving as the first presi-dent of the Salt Lake Temple at the time. He often stayed late into the evening to finish his work.

President Snow's granddaughter Allie Young Pond loved to visit him at his office. In those days, family members of the temple presi-dent were allowed to visit him there. They were not allowed to go through the entire temple, however, until they were old enough and

had been found worthy and ready to make the sacred temple covenants. Read what Allie wrote about that night:

"One evening while I was visiting Grandpa Snow in his room in the Salt Lake Temple, I remained until the doorkeepers had gone and the night-watchmen had not yet come in. Grandpa said he would take me to the main front entrance and let me out that way. He got his bunch of keys from his dresser. After we left his room and while we were still in the large corridor leading into the celestial room, I was walking several steps ahead of grandpa when he stopped me and said: 'Wait a moment, Allie, I want to tell you something. It was right here that the Lord Jesus Christ appeared to me at the time of the death of President Woodruff. He instructed me to go right ahead and reorganize the First Presidency of the Church at once and not wait as had been done after the death of the previous presidents. I was to succeed President Woodruff' [as president of the Church].

"Then grandpa came a step nearer and held out his left hand and said: 'He stood right here, about three feet above the floor. It looked as though He stood on a plate of solid Gold.'

"Grandpa told me what a glorious personage the Savior is and described His hands, feet, countenance and beautiful white robes, all of which were of such a glory of whiteness and brightness that he could hardly gaze upon Him.

"Then he came another step nearer and put his right hand on my head and said: 'Now granddaughter, I want you to remember that this is the testimony of your grandfather, that he told you with his own lips that he actually saw the Savior, here in the Temple, and talked with Him face to face.'"[1]

Can you imagine the humility and reverence you would feel to walk the same halls the Savior walked? You can understand that to enter the temple and to partake of its spirit and to participate in its ordinances one must be personally prepared and worthy. Young women who follow the standards of personal worthiness will find themselves in harmony with temple worthiness guidelines.

Elizabeth, you can be guided toward the temple as you live those standards. Do you remember what they are? I am listing them here just for fun and for your convenience and review. I think each one of us could review these standards often. It is a great checklist!

☐ I pray in private daily.
☐ I read the scriptures regularly.
☐ I seek the guidance of the Spirit.
☐ I honor my father and mother.
☐ I am morally clean.
☐ I obey the Word of Wisdom, including not using tobacco, alcoholic drinks, coffee, tea, or harmful drugs.
☐ I am honest in thought, word, and action.
☐ I pay my tithes and offerings.
☐ I practice the law of the fast.
☐ I respect and support the priesthood.
☐ I obey the laws of the land.
☐ I apply the principles of repentance and forgiveness.
☐ I help make my family life better.

Aren't you glad you are not left on your own to keep these high standards? There are parents and Church leaders who will teach you and walk with you. With them and with good friends—if you are blessed to have that kind of friends—you can follow the Savior. You can also have the constant companionship of the Holy Ghost to help you stay on the straight and narrow path.

Standards of personal worthiness prepare you for the temple recommend interview. As you live these standards you will be preparing to make and keep sacred covenants in the house of the Lord.

When you go to the temple for the first time you will dress in sacred white clothing. All dressed in white, in a special room of the temple, the temple matron (who is the wife of the temple president or the wife of one of his counselors) speaks to sisters prior to their receiving the endowment. She will teach you important things you

need to understand about the temple and she will remind you that this is the day you've been preparing for during your years in the Young Women program. This is what you were talking about as you stood to repeat the theme each Sunday. This is the day you were talking about when you said: "We will be prepared to make and keep sacred covenants, receive the ordinances of the temple, and enjoy the blessings of exaltation."

The temple matron will discuss with sisters the covenants they are about to make with Heavenly Father as they receive the temple endowment. It is a sweet, holy day in the life of a young woman prepared. On this day in the temple, you come closer to heaven than you have ever been before.

From that point on you will have special and sacred goals written in your heart. As you go back to the temple you will be reminded of those commitments you made. In your daily living you will want to renew your efforts to live in the Lord's way. Making temple covenants is the vision of faithful girls in the Church. They know that in the temple, families are bound and sealed together forever.

Dear, sweet friend, all that you do to be worthy to partake of temple blessings is so very much worth it. What temple is nearest to your home? Have you ever been there for proxy baptisms? If you have, what are some of your memories of that sacred occasion? What temple do you want to be married in? Will it be hard, where you live, to find a young man who is worthy to take you to the temple when you marry? Please share your feelings about what I have written to you in this letter. I would love to know how you feel about the temple.

That our ties of friendship will be eternal is my fond hope.

Your friend

chapter twenty-one

Mothers, Keepers of the Springs

A loving, nurturing nature

Dear Elizabeth,

I loved what you wrote to me about your feelings regarding the temple. How blessed you are to have one not too far away! I'm also glad to hear that you have been thinking about what you want to be when you grow up. I love you and have great faith in your abilities and in your future. Your future is the future of the world, for you can be one to nurture the generations yet unborn. You can do this at church, in the neighborhood, and in your own home. I hope that in all your planning you will turn your heart to the importance of the family.

There are, in the world, anti-family forces with strong voices. You will be exposed to their false messages. Along with your parents, I too am concerned about what you hear, read in print, and see acted out on screen. The media has the power to condone, even promote, anti-family messages by what they print, what they show, and how they

show it. There are those who would have us choose abortion over babies, advancing a career over motherhood, and, in place of parents, call for government-sponsored day care and after-school programs to watch over what they term "burdensome" children.

Elizabeth, I believe that this message is wrong. We know that human life is sacred, that children need mothers to nurture, nourish, and teach them, and that they need fathers to love them, to provide for them, and to protect the family unit.

May I share a story told by Peter Marshall:

"Once upon a time, there was a town nestled at the foot of a mountain range where it was sheltered from wind and storms. High up in the hills above the little village, a quiet forest dweller took it upon himself to be the Keeper of the Springs. He patrolled the hills and wherever he found a spring he cleaned its brown pool of silt and fallen leaves of mud and mold and took away from the spring all foreign matter, so that the water which bubbled up through the sand ran down clean and cold and pure. But the City Council was a group of hard-headed, hard boiled business men. They scanned the civic budget and found in it, the salary of the Keeper of the Springs. Said the Keeper of the Purse: 'Why should we pay this romance ranger? We never see him; he is not necessary to our town's work life. If we build a reservoir just above the town, we can dispense with his services and save his salary.' Therefore, the City Council voted to dispense with the unnecessary cost of the Keeper of the Springs, and to build a cement reservoir.

"So the Keeper of the Springs no longer visited the brown pools but watched from the heights while they built the reservoir. When it was finished it soon filled up with water to be sure, but the water did not seem to be the same. It did not seem to be as clean, and a green scum soon befouled its stagnant surface. There were constant troubles with the delicate machinery of the mills, for it was often clogged with slime, and the swans found another home above the town.

"At last, an epidemic raged, and the clammy, yellow fingers of

sickness reached every home in every street and lane. The City Council met again. Sorrowfully, it faced the city's plight, and frankly it acknowledged the mistake of the dismissal of the Keeper of the Springs.

"They sought him out high in the hills, and begged him to return to his former joyous labor. Gladly he agreed, and began once more to make his rounds. It was not long until pure water came lilting down under tunnels of ferns and mosses and to sparkle in the cleansed reservoir."[1]

My dear Elizabeth, there will always be need for the Keeper of the Springs! Mothers are keepers of the springs, and the springs of which I speak are families. In many ways, the homes and families of our world are being more polluted than the mountain spring of the story.

The clammy yellow fingers of moral sickness will reach into every home, every street, and every life unless we are vigilant and prepared to create and defend strong homes. Motherhood is the noblest calling in life. It is something to prepare for with great care.

We, as daughters of God, must plan and prepare to keep the headwaters of the family—the home—clear and clean, so that strong, safe, productive boys and girls may flow freely from them.

I pray that you will be true to family values, true to that noble errand of motherhood which is given to women. It is something to prepare for with great care. For it is given to wives and husbands to guard their own homes and families and then to be an influence in their larger communities.

I would like to offer some suggestions for being a great Keeper of the Springs, Elizabeth. We must treasure traditional family values. The solutions to the world's troubles, which are like the polluted reservoir of the story, include the daily, individual attention given by parents who are willing to invest their best time and efforts. Happiness and security comes in families with a father and mother who are married and committed to each other, committed to nurturing children and raising them to be caring, productive adults.

Elizabeth, I hope you will become an accomplished, capable, woman and never apologize for following the time-proven traditions that have made our society strong. Make the traditions of vigilant watch care over home and family your number one priority. May you aspire to noble motherhood as your greatest calling and not succumb to the demeaning alternative voices of those who would destroy families.

May you marry a man of learning and understanding who will stand prepared to fulfill his duty as provider and protector in the family setting. May you find and fall in love with a young man who willingly embraces his position of responsibility in his future family.

May you believe what the First Presidency and the Quorum of the Twelve Apostles say in the Proclamation on the Family, that marriage between a man and a woman and fidelity in that marriage is the truest safeguard for home and family. You must model moral integrity before and after marriage. There is no viable substitute for the traditional moral values that keep families strong.

No society ever became great by lowering its moral standards. Politically correct is not always morally correct! We need keepers of the springs who will realize that what is socially acceptable in our world today may not be morally right. To be great, we must be good!

Turn your heart to the family. If keepers of the springs desert their posts or are unfaithful to their responsibilities, the future outlook for this world will be bleak indeed. How large will your sphere of influence be and how far will it reach? You decide. It is up to you.

Develop faith in the Lord Jesus Christ, understand the relationship between choice and accountability, do good works, live a life of integrity, and realize that *parents* are responsible for the nurture and stability of families, not governments or agencies.

I love what Elder Neal A. Maxwell has said about the great role of women, "When the real history of mankind is fully disclosed, will it feature the echoes of gunfire or the shaping sound of lullabies? The great armistices made by military men or the peacemaking of women

in homes and in neighborhoods? Will what happened in cradles and kitchens prove to be more controlling than what happened in congresses? When the surf of the centuries has made the great pyramids so much sand, the everlasting family will still be standing."[2] This must be so. We, as women, must make it so. It is up to us!

Turning your heart to the family can be your ideal, Elizabeth. My own experience convinces me of the supreme value of this ideal. For more than thirty years now I have devoted my life to my husband and family of seven sons. How grateful I am for the blessing and opportunity to be a keeper of one little spring. With all that I could have chosen to do, with whatever ability and talent I have, I doubt that anything else I would have chosen could have more long-term impact in our society than these seven stalwart sons who have been scattered across this world from Russia to Wall Street, Guatemala to Great Britain, Belgium to Brazil, even Africa, doing good for mankind.

Now these seven sons, products of our family, are getting married to wonderful, accomplished young women. They are producing incomes and becoming fathers. As couples, married for eternity in the temple, they are establishing families of their own, and a new generation of keepers of the springs is beginning.

In my own experience, limited as it may be, I have come to believe that it is in the family where we find our greatest satisfaction, our fulfillment, our peace, our joy, and our intergenerational influence.

As a creator and defender of a family, as a mother, I believe I am involved in something everlasting. I believe the influence of a mother will live on through her sons and her daughters and future generations. Our posterity will bless many lives and, in the end, they will bless the life of the mother because she was a keeper of the springs.

With love,

Your friend

Mothers, keepers of the springs

P. S. What are your thoughts about families? Do your ideas differ from what the world teaches? How has your own family experience influenced your feelings? I look forward to your next letter.

chapter twenty-two

Keep Thyself Pure

walk in paths of virtue

Dear Elizabeth,

In your last letter you asked about a memorable moment in my life when I was about your age. There truly are highlights that stand apart as significant. One such moment in my life was a personal meeting with President David O. McKay. When I was in college, not much older than you, I received an invitation to meet with the president of the Church, along with a group of other young people. I remember my great feelings of unpreparedness for such an interview, but I also remember thinking how marvelous it would be if I could sit close to him and receive his personal counsel to me.

I was determined to be spiritually prepared for this special visit. With a prayer in my heart, I read my scriptures all the way from Provo to Salt Lake City, typical of the "cramming" style of a college student! It must have worked because the meeting was wonderful. As we

arrived at President McKay's apartment at the Hotel Utah, several of the apostles were leaving and they stopped to greet us, and then, Elizabeth, I met the prophet.

He invited us to sit with him on the couch and he took my youthful hand in his large, warm prophet's hand for the duration of the meeting. I will forever remember the great warmth and love I felt in his presence as he talked with us.

All too soon the visit ended, and I realized that there had been no personal advice for any of us. In fact, the words of the meeting have left my memory; but priorities became very clear that day. I had heard the prophet teach principles from the pulpit, and on this day I understood that when the prophet speaks he is speaking to me—and to you. Ever since then I have listened carefully to the words of the prophet when he speaks because I know his words give sure guidance for our lives.

Many years later, about thirty to be exact, I once again was invited to visit the prophet, the president of the Church. This time it was President Gordon B. Hinckley. I was with only one other person this time. It was my best friend, my beloved husband, Stephen. We had spent our lives listening carefully to the words of the prophets and trying our best to follow their counsel to us. On this visit I did not sit next to the prophet on the couch, but instead I sat across the desk from him with my husband at my side. We had a wonderful visit, which ended with a most remarkable request. He asked me to serve as the president of the Young Women of the Church. Can you imagine how my heart swelled with immeasurable humility at the thought of being given such a sacred trust?

And then the prophet of God told me how wonderful the young women of the Church are and how much Heavenly Father loves them. That includes you, Elizabeth.

From that day on I have had a special love for you and a special concern for your well-being. I have wanted you to know how very much you are loved and how very much your Heavenly Father wants

you to be successful in your life's mission. He wants you to keep yourself clean and pure. He wants you to live a virtuous life even though our world is polluted with immorality and unworthy enticements. Heavenly Father knows you. He knows the valiant spirit you came to earth with. He knows you can be strong in the face of temptations and those opposing voices that entice you to leave the path of goodness. He promises to help you as you seek His help. But you must first invite Him. Invite Him through prayer. Invite Him by living a worthy life. Invite Him to speak to you as you read His word in scripture. Listen to His promptings and direction through that still, small voice called the Holy Ghost. And follow the prophet!

President Hinckley has taught, "The Lord has made it clear, and the experience of centuries has confirmed it, that happiness lies not in immorality, but rather in abstinence. The voice of the Church to which you belong is a voice pleading for virtue. . . . It is a voice declaring that sexual transgression is a sin. It is contrary to the will of the Lord. It is contrary to the teachings of the Church. It is contrary to the happiness and well-being of those who indulge in it.

"You should recognize, you *must* recognize, that both experience and divine wisdom dictate virtue and moral cleanliness as the way that leads to strength of character, peace in the heart, and happiness in life."[1]

Paul put it plainly and simply when he said, "Keep thyself pure" (1 Timothy 5:22). I believe that. And being "pure" includes not touching another person in the private, sacred parts of their body, with clothes on or off. It includes keeping your mind pure and free from pornographic images. You are in charge of your mind and your body. You have a sacred responsibility to keep them pure.

When you become married, you are then authorized to be blessed with close and intimate expressions of love with your husband. The Lord desires you to draw close to your husband to create children and to strengthen the bonds of marriage and commitment to each other.

Remember, the key is *after marriage*. (That's hardly what the soap operas or other T. V. shows or most movies teach, is it?)

There are some precious and beloved daughters of Heavenly Father who have been victims of abuse that they did not initiate. They are not unclean before God in this circumstance, and their bishops can help them understand this. The bishop can help them know with assurance how much Heavenly Father loves them. In fact, I believe that the Lord has a very special love for these beloved daughters, and He will carry for them the difficult burden they worry about. We read about this in Alma 7:11: "And he [Christ] shall go forth, suffering pains and afflictions and temptations of every kind; and this that the word might be fulfilled which saith he will take upon him the pains and the sicknesses of his people." It is true. Christ not only took upon Himself our sins and allows us to repent of them, but He also carries our sorrows and our pains. We can turn them over to our beloved Savior. How I love Him.

Dear Elizabeth, this is pretty heavy material. But it is something that is important to understand and believe. I pray for you and for every young woman in this Church that you will walk in virtue and purity and confidence before God.

Would you feel worthy to visit with the prophet? Have you had some tender thoughts about personal purity as you have read this letter? I hope that you would be willing to share them with me.

With love and confidence in your ability to do what is right at all times, in all things, and in all places.

Your loving sister

chapter twenty-three

Come unto Jesus

. . . and we're all invited

Dear Elizabeth,

Thank you for the sweet letter. I will treasure your tender thoughts expressed.

Since it will soon be the Easter season, I can't help but rejoice in the most meaningful invitation ever extended to mankind. It is the invitation to come unto Christ. And we're all invited!

The scriptures are filled with that glorious invitation, which is beautifully summarized in this hymn:

> Come unto Jesus from ev'ry nation,
> From ev'ry land and isle of the sea.
> Unto the high and lowly in station,
> Ever he calls, "Come to me, to me."[1]

The Savior extends His generous invitation simply because He

loves us and He knows we need Him. He can help us and heal us. He understands us because of His own experiences. We want to come unto Christ because it is only in Him and through Him that we can return to the Father.

Elizabeth, could I share with you a simple thing that happened many years ago that I have always remembered because it caused me to think about the Savior's mission. Although it was just a childish incident, it has some meaning. It happened when our twins were only about five years old. They were just learning to ride their bicycles. As I glanced out the window, I saw them speeding down the street on their bikes going very fast! Perhaps they were going a little too fast for their level of ability because all of a sudden Adam had a terrible crash! He was tangled up in the wreck, and all I could see was a twist of handlebars and tires and arms and legs. His little twin brother, Aaron, saw the whole thing happen and immediately he skidded to a stop and jumped off his bike. He threw it down and ran to the aid of his brother whom he loved so much. These little twins truly were of one heart. If one hurt, so did the other. If one got tickled, they both laughed. If one started a sentence, the other could finish it. What one felt, the other did also. So it was painful for Aaron to see Adam crash! Adam was a mess. He had skinned knees, he was bleeding from a head wound, his pride was damaged, and he was crying. In a fairly gentle five-year-old way, Aaron helped his brother get untangled from the crash, he checked out the wounds, and then he did the dearest thing. He picked his brother up and carried him home. Or tried to. This wasn't easy because they were the same size, but he tried. And as he struggled and lifted and half-dragged, half-carried his brother along, they finally reached the front porch. By this time, Adam, the injured one, was no longer crying, but Aaron, the rescuer, was. When asked, "Why are you crying, Aaron?" he said simply, "Because Adam hurts." And so he had brought him home to help, home to someone who knew what to do, to someone who could cleanse the wounds, bind them up, and make it better. Home to love.

Just as one twin helped his brother in need, so might we all be lifted, helped, even carried at times by our beloved Savior, the Lord Jesus Christ. He feels what we feel; He knows our hearts. It was His mission to wipe away our tears, cleanse our wounds, and bless us with His healing power. He can carry us home to our Heavenly Father with the strength of His matchless love.

Elizabeth, I am sure that it pleases the Lord when we, His children, reach out to one another, to give help along the way, and to bring another closer to Christ. He wants us to "mourn with those that mourn; . . . comfort those that stand in need of comfort" (Mosiah 18:9).

The words of Susan Evans McCloud say it well:

> Savior, may I learn to love thee,
> Walk the path that thou hast shown,
> Pause to help and lift another,
> Finding strength beyond my own. . . .
>
> I would be my brother's keeper;
> I would learn the healer's art.
> To the wounded and the weary
> I would show a gentle heart. . . .
>
> Savior, may I love my brother
> As I know thou lovest me,
> Find in thee my strength, my beacon,
> For thy servant I would be.[2]

I love it that young girls understand the doctrines and ordinances of the Church. For example, when we asked some young women what they liked about sacrament meeting one said, "The sacrament, because it reminds me of Jesus and all He did for me." Another said, "I never come away with an empty heart. I love taking the sacrament." When asked how often they prayed, many said "morning and night." Along with their own personal preparation, these young

women are blessing lives of others. I am sure that you are too, Elizabeth.

May I share a letter from a grateful recipient of the loving service of young women like you. He wrote:

"The young women [of my ward] very literally saved my life. I was a young bishop, just twenty-nine, the father of four beautiful little girls, including a small baby, when Heavenly Father called my wife home to Him. As I met with each of our little girls and asked them what impact this change would mean to them, the concerns of six-year-old Emily, the oldest of the four, were many including, 'Who is going to comb and curl my hair for church and put ribbons and clips in it?' That was a good question to me as well. Who? I was consumed with the idea that life would be as 'normal' as possible for all of us—which meant that I would have to learn a whole new way of life. I was their father, and I was going to be *the* only parent. I realized that I was not equipped with the motherly skill levels I needed. I called upon the young women of the ward to train me to be able to satisfy at least the needs of hair care. They came to my home, numerous times, to begin my training. They even showed me how to care for my six-month-old Natalie as far as washing her hair without so much trauma. By the time I 'graduated,' I could whip up a mean (but simple) hairdo. Much more than the skill, those young women gave me confidence as a father of daughters that I could love them, care for them, be there for them, no matter how the rest of my life continued."[3]

Dear sweet friend, I want you to know of my testimony of the Savior, Jesus Christ. I know that as we accept the invitation to come unto Christ, we will find that He can heal all wounds. He can lift our burdens and carry them for us, and we can feel "encircled about eternally in the arms of his love" (2 Nephi 1:15).

It would be a special privilege for me to read your testimony if you would ever feel inspired to share it.

write back soon!

Thanks, Elizabeth, for your continuing friendship and your willingness to keep reading my letters to you, even if I am a little "older sister." You are loved!

Your friend

chapter twenty-four

And We Love Him

"we love Him, because He first loved us"

Dear Elizabeth,

Today I heard a beautiful young woman pray. The expressions came from her heart. In her prayer, she said, "We love thee, Heavenly Father," just as we say in the Young Women theme each week. The expression of love was tender and heartfelt, I could tell by her spirit. I watched as this girl showed by her actions that she loved her Father in Heaven.

The Savior taught, "As I have loved you, love one another." Katie understood what this teaching meant; you could tell it by the way she lived her life and even by the way she worked. She looked forward to her job each day after school. No, it wasn't selling the latest fashions at the boutique in the mall or serving customers at the video shop. This was a job with heart. For two years Katie helped Farah, who was severely handicapped, enjoy life a little more.

Together they sang, went shopping, read stories, and studied scriptures. They played games and took field trips. Sometimes they had sleepovers together so Farah's family could have a break. Katie dressed Farah, helped her with her personal grooming, and cared for her physical needs.

When it was time for Katie to choose a Laurel project, her thoughts turned to Farah. She wanted to think of something special that she could do for her. She searched for a way to express her love for her good friend. In Young Women activities they had done much with family history, and it was on her mind in a major way. So Katie decided to make a Book of Remembrance for Farah. She collected pictures and stories and family histories, all part of Farah's life story. In her spare time she put the book together into a beautiful treasure for Farah to enjoy.

Seeing her friend happy made Katie happy. She was loved and blessed and wanted others to feel the same way. She lived the Savior's teaching: "As I have loved you, love one another."

On December 30, Katie was home with her brother, planning to join the rest of the family the next day to celebrate New Year's Eve. She had just completed her own autobiography as part of a school assignment and had it packed to take with her to share with her family for their holiday time together. When she left the house the next morning, she left a note lying on top of her scriptures at the side of her bed. Perhaps it was part of her school writing project. It was just one paragraph. She had written:

"If it were my last day on earth this is the record I would leave: Make each day meaningful. Be there for others. Stay close to the Lord. Gain all the knowledge you can about the scriptures, the gospel, the creations of the Lord. Smile often, give of yourself, even if at times you feel you have nothing left to give. And always remember Christ for His example and His atonement, and strive each day to be like Him."

The day she wrote those words was Katie's last day on earth. The

next day, as she rode with her brother to join the family to celebrate the New Year, Katie was killed in a car accident. Surely, when she met her Heavenly Father, He knew that Katie loved Him. She showed her love for Him by the way she loved His other children.

We sing:

> As I have loved you,
> Love one another
> This new commandment:
> Love one another.
> By this shall men know
> Ye are my disciples,
> If ye have love
> One to another.[1]

The February 1999 *New Era* reported the story of four girls who relied on their Savior's love when they were stranded in a terrible storm as they headed back to college after the Thanksgiving holiday.

"About 15 miles north of Elko, Nevada, is a stretch of highway dotted with signs warning motorists not to pick up hitchhikers because of a prison facility nearby. To four college students traveling from Provo, Utah, to San Francisco, these signs were a bit unsettling. My roommates and I were certainly glad to cruise by them on our way to California's Bay Area for Thanksgiving weekend. We didn't think twice about the signs until four days later on our way back to Provo. It was then that our car suddenly stopped precisely 10 yards north of one of those ominous blue signs.

"Our first instincts were to flag down another car and ask for a ride back to Elko. But images of escaped convicts kept us locked inside the car. It was four in the afternoon, it was snowing, and it would definitely be dark and very cold within the hour. We needed help fast but were too afraid to even get out of the car. We offered a short prayer, and 30 minutes later a man driving a snowplow stopped

and radioed the police for us. A young officer piled us into his car, called a tow truck, and dropped us off at a motel in Elko.

"We soon got over our fears and realized how blessed we were to get off the highway unharmed and be in a safe, warm motel room. Our only problem now was getting back to Provo. Each of us dialed home collect, expecting that our parents would wire money for bus tickets or a rental car. We were surprised when each set of parents immediately offered to drive to Elko and get us.

"Even for the closest set of parents, this meant a three-hour drive to Elko and a four-hour drive back to Provo. It meant disrupting work schedules and finding baby-sitters for the other children. Eventually we decided that it would be best for Jenni's mom and grandpa to drive down to get us. Relieved, we went to bed and expected to see Jenni's mom by noon the next day.

"Things didn't go quite as planned. Overnight the snow storm had worsened, and the roads were terrible. Despite leaving Salt Lake City at 10:00 A.M., Jenni's mom didn't get to us until four that afternoon. The roads back were equally icy, and a typically four-hour drive took six hours. Still, Jenni's mom and grandpa never uttered a word of complaint during the entire drive home. They were only happy to help and grateful that we would be home soon.

"No matter where we had been stranded, any of our parents would have done all they could to bring us back home. The same is true of our heavenly parents. And our Heavenly Father will take us all the way home, not just to a safe resting place. No matter how lost or confused we may be, we need only to make a humble call to our Heavenly Father, promising to heed His words, and He will lead us back.

". . . I knew that my Heavenly Father would always help me. He does so without complaint, for He is happy just to know that I am on my way home and will soon be safe in His arms."[2]

That's the way it is with love. To express it, you have to do something. You have to be on the road back home, toward heaven.

Always remember to *tell* Heavenly Father you love Him when you talk to Him in prayer. Never miss an opportunity to *show* Him you love Him by the love you give to others, especially your mother and father and others in your family.

For truly, "Inasmuch as ye have done it unto one of the least of these my brethren, ye have done it unto me" (Matthew 25:40). I believe that with all my heart. Do you, Liz? Have you had any experiences with showing love to another? Please write to me about this. I'm always inspired by loving acts of service.

Your friend

chapter twenty-five

Follow the Leader

"Lead me, guide me, walk beside me"

Dear Liz,

Did you know that in Israel they still care for sheep the same way they did two thousand years ago when Jesus walked among men? Each evening at sundown, shepherds bring their small flocks of sheep to a common enclosure where they are secured against the wolves and other predators that roam the fields. A single shepherd guards the gate until morning, when the shepherds come to the enclosure one by one and call to their sheep, by name. The sheep will not respond to the voice of a stranger, but will leave the enclosure only in the care of their true shepherd, confident because the shepherd knows their names and they know his voice. This is described in John 10:2–5. "But he that entereth in by the door is the shepherd of the sheep. To him the porter openeth; and the sheep hear his voice: and he calleth his own sheep by name, and leadeth them out. And when he putteth

forth his own sheep, he goeth before them, and the sheep follow him: for they know his voice. And a stranger will they not follow, but will flee from him: for they know not the voice of strangers."

There is a scripture in 1 John 4:19 that states, "We love him, because he first loved us." Love is the key to opening the door of leadership. Love for those we would lead and love for Him who loved us first, our Savior, Jesus Christ. To lead others then, one must first be a follower, a follower of the perfect leader, the Good Shepherd.

Elizabeth, there are calls for leadership all around us in today's world: in the school you attend, with your friends, at home, and at church. I believe that all young women today have some responsibility to be leaders. Wow, that's a pretty bold statement, isn't it? But I really believe that. It is not good for us to think that what we say and what we do doesn't really matter. In today's world, we do not have the luxury of saying that we will let someone else do it, or that we are too busy, or we don't know how, or we aren't interested. We must all realize that, like it or not, we have been given a leadership responsibility by virtue of being a member of God's true Church and because we live in this time and season of the world's history. That's a very awesome and daunting idea.

I really do think that you can use your God-given abilities to motivate, inspire, and build others. Your leadership talents can, and will, and must bless others. And I believe that as you, and other young women like you, assume this leadership responsibility you will be blessed and magnified, and the part of the world in which you live will be better for your having been there.

Natalia is a young woman whose faith in a newfound religion caused her to use leadership skills she had no idea she had. Would you like to know her story, Elizabeth? Well, here it is: At the young age of fifteen, Natalia was an exchange student from the Ukraine in the home of an LDS family in Illinois when she received a testimony of the gospel of Jesus Christ and was baptized on her sixteenth birthday.

Soon after her baptism it was time for her to return home to the Ukraine. Of this experience she writes:

"I knew I would be the only member of the Church in my home-town of Cherkassy, Ukraine, a city of about 350,000. I remember my flight home. I was very scared and depressed because I had been a member of the Church for just four months and I just couldn't imagine that I would go back to a place where there was no church. I wouldn't be able to take the sacrament and things like that. I wanted to support my testimony, and I prayed to God so hard. While I was flying and reading the Book of Mormon, I just felt the Spirit and it kind of comforted me.

"A week after being home I was praying and it was fasting time and I was fasting. Then a thought came to my mind, 'Why don't you just start the gospel with your family?'

"I found out the steps that needed to be taken for the Church to be recognized in Cherkassy. With the Lord's help, I succeeded in get-ting a professor at the university and the head counselor of my school to not only sign the necessary petition, but also agree to let the missionaries come and teach their students."[1]

What a remarkable thing she did!

This young girl, about your age, exhibited great leadership in making it possible to get the gospel message to the people of her city. When the missionaries came, there was Natalia, practically waiting at the gates of the city, to welcome them and make it possible for them to do their important work!

It amazes me the things that young and inexperienced girls can accomplish as they step up and assume a leadership role!

Elise is another girl who did remarkable things because she dared to take a stand. That is what leadership is! She is from Arkansas. She said, "One of the things that this Church has taught me is to stand up for what is right despite what people think."

While watching a movie with her little sister, Elise was disap-pointed in what was depicted on the screen and decided she could not

trust Hollywood. So for her Laurel project, Elise drafted a letter and petition urging others to support family movies. With the help of ward members, Elise posted her letter on the Internet. To date she has collected 87,378 signatures. By her efforts Elise hopes to prove to Hollywood producers that there is a market and demand for edited, refined media.

I am sure that you have had an opportunity to be a leader, Liz. In your home, or elsewhere, whether formally called by a bishop, or elected by peers, there are opportunities for each one of us to be a leader for truth and righteousness. Tell me about a time in your life when you took on a leadership role. How did it make you feel? Were you able to make a difference? Will you continue to develop your leadership ability? Write all about it in your next letter.

We're depending on you!

Your friend

chapter twenty-six

The Joy of Womanhood

Grateful daughters of God

Dear Elizabeth,

Remember when I wrote my first letter to you? I was so excited about the new baby girl who had just been born into our family. Well, Liz, I want you to know that I am also excited for you and all the possibilities that life has in store for you. You will have amazing opportunities to make a real difference in our world because you are a beloved daughter of God.

I want you to really understand that it is a remarkable blessing to be a daughter of God today! We have the fulness of the gospel of Jesus Christ. We are blessed to have the priesthood restored to the earth. We are led by a prophet of God who holds all of the priesthood keys. I love and honor President Gordon B. Hinckley and all of our brethren who bear the priesthood worthily.

As I have already told you, I am inspired by the lives of good and faithful women. You know by now that *I* know that our Heavenly Father loves His daughters very much. From the beginning of time

149

the Lord has placed significant trust in them. He has sent us to earth for such a time as this to perform a grand and glorious mission. Remember what I showed you from the Doctrine and Covenants about the "noble and great ones"? "Even before they were born, they, with many others, received their first lessons in the world of spirits and were prepared to come forth in the due time of the Lord to labor in his vineyard for the salvation of the souls of men" (D&C 138:56). What a wonderful vision that gives us of our purpose on earth! But Liz, we must always remember that where much is given, much is required. Our Heavenly Father asks His daughters to walk in virtue, to live in righteousness, so that we can fulfill our life's mission and His purposes. He wants us to be successful, and He will help us as we seek His help.

That women were born into this earth female was determined long before mortal birth, as were the divine differences of males and females. I love the clarity of the teachings of the First Presidency and the Quorum of the Twelve in the Proclamation on the Family. They state: "Gender is an essential characteristic of individual premortal, mortal, and eternal identity and purpose." From that statement we are taught that every girl was feminine and female in spirit long before her mortal birth.

God sent women to earth with some qualities in extra capacity. President Faust observed that femininity "is the divine adornment of humanity. It finds expression in your . . . capacity to love, your spirituality, delicacy, radiance, sensitivity, creativity, charm, graciousness, gentleness, dignity, and quiet strength. It is manifest differently in each girl or woman, but each . . . possesses it. Femininity is part of your inner beauty."[1]

Our outward appearance is a reflection of what we are inside. Our lives reflect that for which we seek. If, with all our hearts, we truly seek to know the Savior and be more like Him, we shall be, for He is our divine, eternal Brother. But He is more than that. He is our

precious Savior, our dear Redeemer. I ask, with Alma of old, "Have ye received his image in your countenances?" (Alma 5:14).

Liz, you can recognize young women who are grateful to be daughters of God by their outward appearance. They understand their stewardship over their bodies and treat them with dignity. They care for their bodies as they would a holy temple, for they understand the Lord's teaching: "Know ye not that ye are the temple of God, and that the Spirit of God dwelleth in you?" (1 Corinthians 3:16). Young Women who love God would never abuse or deface a temple with graffiti. Nor would they throw open the doors of that holy, dedicated edifice and invite the world to look on. How even more sacred is the body, for it was not made by man. It was created by God. We are the stewards, the keepers of the cleanliness and purity with which it came from heaven. "If any man defile the temple of God, him shall God destroy, for the temple of God is holy, which temple ye are" (1 Corinthians 3:17).

Grateful daughters of God guard their bodies carefully, for they know they are the wellspring of life and they reverence life. They don't uncover their bodies to find favor with the world. They walk in modesty to be in favor with their Father in Heaven. They know He loves them dearly.

You can recognize young women who are grateful to be daughters of God by their attitudes. They know that the errand of angels is given to women, and they desire to be on God's errand, to love His children and minister to them; to teach them the doctrines of salvation; to call them to repentance; to save them in perilous circumstances; to guide them in the performance of His work; to deliver His messages. They understand that they can bless their Father's children in their homes and neighborhoods and beyond. Young women who are grateful to be daughters of God bring glory to His name.

You can recognize young women who are grateful to be daughters of God by their abilities. They fulfill their divine potential and magnify their God-given gifts. They are capable, strong young women

who bless families, serve others, and understand that the glory of God is intelligence. They are young women who embrace enduring virtues in order to be all our Father needs them to be. The prophet Jacob spoke of some of those virtues when he said their "feelings are exceedingly tender and chaste and delicate before God, which thing is pleasing unto God" (Jacob 2:7).

Grateful daughters of God love Him and will teach others to love Him without reservation and without resentment. They will grow up to be like the mothers of Helaman's youthful army who had great faith and "had been taught by their mothers, that if they did not doubt, God would deliver them" (Alma 56:47).

Elizabeth, when you observe kind and gentle mothers in action, you will see women of great strength. You will observe that their families can feel a spirit of love and respect and safety when they are near her as she seeks the companionship of the Holy Ghost and the guidance of His Spirit. You will see that they are blessed by her wisdom and good judgment. The husbands and children, whose lives these mothers bless, will contribute to the stability of societies all over this world. Grateful daughters of God learn truths from their mothers and grandmothers. They teach their daughters the joyful art of creating a home. They seek fine educations for their children and have a thirst for knowledge themselves. They help their children develop skills they can use in serving others. They know that the way they have chosen is not the easy way, but they know it is absolutely worth their finest efforts. That is the kind of mother you can become, Elizabeth!

They understand what Elder Neal A. Maxwell meant as he said: "When the real history of mankind is fully disclosed, will it feature the echoes of gunfire or the shaping sound of lullabies? The great armistices made by military men or the peacemaking of women in homes and in neighborhoods? Will what happened in cradles and kitchens prove to be more controlling than what happened in

congresses?"[2] I've shared that with you in another letter, but it is such a profound truth that I thought I would repeat it again today.

Grateful daughters of God know that it is the nurturing nature of women that can bring everlasting blessings, and they live to cultivate this divine attribute. Surely when a woman reverences motherhood, her children will arise up and call her blessed (Proverbs 31:28).

Elizabeth, always remember that women of God can never be like women of the world. The world has enough women who are tough; we need women who are tender. There are enough women who are coarse; we need women who are kind. There are enough women who are rude; we need women who are refined. We have enough women of fame and fortune; we need more women of faith. We have enough greed; we need more goodness. We have enough vanity; we need more virtue. We have enough popularity; we need more purity.

Oh, Elizabeth, how I pray that every young woman will grow up to be all the wonderful things she is meant to be. I hope that as a daughter of God you honor the priesthood and sustain worthy priesthood holders. I hope you understand your own great capacity for strength in the timeless virtues that some would scoff at in a modern, liberated world for women.

May you understand the great potential for good you inherited from your heavenly home. We, as women, must nourish our gentleness, our nurturing nature, our innate spirituality and sensitivity, and our bright minds. Celebrate the fact that girls are different from boys. Be thankful for the position you have in God's grand plan. And always remember what President Hinckley said, "Woman is God's supreme creation. Only after the earth had been formed, after the day had been separated from the night, after the waters had been divided from the land, after vegetation and animal life had been created, and after man had been placed on the earth, was woman created; and only then was the work pronounced complete and good."[3]

Elizabeth, please write down all that you are and must be, all that you were prepared to be in royal courts on high by God Himself.

write back soon!

Thankfully consider how you can use with gratitude the priceless gifts you have been given to lift others to higher thinking and nobler aspirations.

With love and great expectations for you today and always,

Your friend

_____

_____

_____

_____

_____

_____

_____

_____

_____

_____

_____

_____

❧ Notes ❧

NOTES TO CHAPTER ONE:

1. Ora Pate Stewart, "To a Child" (sheet music), 1964.

2. William Wordsworth, from "Ode on Intimations of Immortality," in *Best-Loved Poems of the LDS People,* comp. Jack M. Lyon, Linda Ririe Gundry, Jay A. Parry, and Devan Jensen (Salt Lake City: Deseret Book, 1996), 62.

NOTES TO CHAPTER TWO:

1. James E. Faust, "Womanhood: The Highest Place of Honor," *Ensign,* May 2000, 96.

2. Gordon B. Hinckley, "Our Responsibility to Our Young Women," *Ensign,* September 1988, 11.

NOTE TO CHAPTER FOUR:

1. Robert Frost, "Stopping by Woods on a Snowy Evening," in *You Come Too* (New York: Holt, Rinehart and Winston Inc., 1959), 24.

NOTE TO CHAPTER FIVE:

1. Parley P. Pratt, *Key Science of Theology* (Salt Lake City: Deseret Book, 1965), 101.

NOTES TO CHAPTER SIX:

1. Shannon D. Jensen, "Stand As a Witness," *New Era,* November 1998, 10.

2. Ezra Taft Benson, "To the 'Youth of the Noble Birthright,'" *Ensign,* May 1986, 43.

3. Gordon B. Hinckley, "A Prophet's Counsel and Prayer," *New Era,* January 2001, 7.

4. Ezra Taft Benson, *The Teachings of Ezra Taft Benson* (Salt Lake City: Bookcraft, 1988), 361.

NOTES TO CHAPTER SEVEN:

1. This story is retold from John Patrick, *The Curious Savage,* New York: Dramatists Play Service Inc., 1951.

2. Author Unknown, "The World Is Mine!" in *Best-Loved Poems of the LDS People,* comp. Jack M. Lyon, Linda Ririe Gundry, Jay A. Parry, and Devan Jensen (Salt Lake City: Deseret Book, 1996), 126–27.

3. Elizabeth Barrett Browning, "Sonnet 43," from *Sonnets from the Portuguese,* in ibid., 211–12.

NOTE TO CHAPTER EIGHT:

1. *Deseret News,* Obituaries, January 26, 1999.

NOTES TO CHAPTER NINE:

1. Carol B. Thomas, "Spiritual Power of Our Baptism," *Ensign,* May 1999, 92.

2. "Nephi's Courage," *Children's Songbook* (Salt Lake City: The Church of Jesus Christ of Latter-day Saints, 1989), 120.

NOTE TO CHAPTER TEN:

1. John McCrae, "In Flanders Field," in *The Best-Loved Poems of the American People* (Garden City, N.J.: Doubleday & Co. Inc, 1936), 429.

NOTES TO CHAPTER ELEVEN:

1. From letter in possession of the General Young Women offices.

2. Robert Frost, "The Road Not Taken," in *You Come Too* (New York: Holt, Rinehart and Winston Inc., 1959), 84.

3. "The Lord Is My Light," *Hymns of The Church of Jesus Christ of Latter-day Saints* (Salt Lake City: The Church of Jesus Christ of Latter-day Saints, 1985), no. 89.

NOTES TO CHAPTER THIRTEEN:

1. Gordon B. Hinckley, "A Chosen Generation," *Ensign*, May 1992, 71.

2. Charles D. McGiver, in *Home Book of Quotations Classical and Modern*, ed. Burton Stevenson (New York: Dodd Mead and Company, 1934), 2193.

3. C. S. Lewis, *Mere Christianity* (New York: Macmillan Publishing Co., 1952), 174.

4. Glenn L. Pace, *Spiritual Plateaus* (Salt Lake City: Deseret Book, 1991), 84–85.

NOTE TO CHAPTER FOURTEEN:

1. In Gordon B. Hinckley, "'Do Ye Even So to Them,'" *Ensign*, December 1991, 5.

NOTE TO CHAPTER FIFTEEN:

1. Gordon B. Hinckley, *Teachings of Gordon B. Hinckley* (Salt Lake City: Deseret Book, 1997), 398.

NOTES TO CHAPTER SEVENTEEN:

1. Kathryn Moore, "Marking My Place," *New Era*, March 2000, 27.

2. "Did You Think to Pray?" *Hymns of The Church of Jesus Christ of Latter-day Saints* (Salt Lake City: The Church of Jesus Christ of Latter-day Saints, 1985), no. 140.

3. This story is retold from *Teachings of Harold B. Lee*, ed. Clyde J. Williams (Salt Lake City: Bookcraft, 1996), 414–15.

NOTE TO CHAPTER NINETEEN:

1. *The Works of Nathaniel Hawthorne* (New York: Houghton, Mifflin and Company, 1851), 3:413–38.

NOTE TO CHAPTER TWENTY:

1. Allie Young Pond, as recorded in Susan Arrington Madsen, *The Lord Needed a Prophet*, 2d ed. (Salt Lake City: Deseret Book, 1996) 83.

NOTES TO CHAPTER TWENTY-ONE:

1. *Peter Marshall's Keeper of the Springs and other Messages from "Mister Jones, Meet the Master,"* Westwood, New York: Fleming H. Revell Company, 9–11.

2. Neal A. Maxwell, "The Women of God," *Ensign*, May 1978, 10–11.

NOTE TO CHAPTER TWENTY-TWO:

1. Gordon B. Hinckley, *The Teachings of Gordon B. Hinckley* (Salt Lake City: Deseret Book, 1997), 48.

NOTES TO CHAPTER TWENTY-THREE:

1. "Come unto Jesus," *Hymns of The Church of Jesus Christ of Latter-day Saints* (Salt Lake City: The Church of Jesus Christ of Latter-day Saints, 1985), no. 117.
2. "Lord, I Would Follow Thee," *Hymns*, no. 220. Used by permission.
3. Personal letter in possession of author. Used by permission.

NOTES TO CHAPTER TWENTY-FOUR:

1. "Love One Another," *Hymns of The Church of Jesus Christ of Latter-day Saints* (Salt Lake City: The Church of Jesus Christ of Latter-day Saints, 1985), no. 308.
2. Janna DeVore, "Please Bring Us Home," *New Era*, February 1999, 26–27.

NOTE TO CHAPTER TWENTY-FIVE:

1. From an interview with the Young Women General Board.

NOTES TO CHAPTER TWENTY-SIX:

1. James E. Faust, "Womanhood: The Highest Place of Honor," *Ensign*, May 2000, 96.
2. Neal A. Maxwell, "The Women of God," *Ensign*, May 1978, 10–11.
3. Gordon B. Hinckley, "Our Responsibility to Our Young Women," *Ensign*, September 1988, 11.

Margaret Dyreng Nadauld was sustained as Young Women General President in October 1997. Her greatest joy and satisfaction has come from being a full-time mother. She graduated from Brigham Young University and taught high school English for two years. She has served on the Relief Society General Board, is a member of the Church Board of Education, and has been a leader in civic organizations. Sister Nadauld was first lady of Weber State University while her husband, Stephen D. Nadauld, served as its president. They are the parents of seven sons.